TIMBER PRESS
POCKET GUIDE TO
Ground Covers

TIMBER PRESS
POCKET GUIDE TO

Ground
Covers

DAVID S. MACKENZIE

TIMBER PRESS

Frontispiece: *Sedum* 'Matrona'

Published in 2006 by

Timber Press, Inc.
The Haseltine Building
133 S.W. Second Avenue, Suite 450
Portland, Oregon 97204-3527, U.S.A.

www.timberpress.com

For contact information regarding editorial, marketing, sales, and distribution in the
United Kingdom, see www.timberpress.co.uk.

Printed through Colorcraft Ltd., Hong Kong

Library of Congress Cataloging-in-Publication Data

MacKenzie, David S.
  Timber Press pocket guide to ground covers / David S. MacKenzie.
        p. cm.
  Includes bibliographical references and index.
  ISBN-13: 978-0-88192-798-6
  ISBN-10: 0-88192-798-8
  1. Ground cover plants. I. Timber Press (Portland, Or.) II. Title.
  SB432.M34 2006
  635.9′64—dc22
                                                      2005033770

A catalog record for this book is also available from the British Library.

Dedication

To all gardeners who value beauty, the environment, and the importance of their leisure time.

Acknowledgments

Thanks again to all those individuals mentioned in *Perennial Ground Covers*, on which this pocket guide is based. Special thanks to those who provided photographs: Tony Avent, Pamela Harper, Master Tag Corporation, Monrovia Nursery, Richard Shiell, Stephen Still, John Trager, and Walters Gardens. Thanks to Linda Willms for an excellent job of editing.

About This Book

This guide to popular and useful perennial ground covers for the North American landscape will help you discover many fascinating plants. Through their versatility and ease of maintenance, these plants will make your gardening experiences all the more pleasant and rewarding.

The plants are arranged alphabetically by scientific name and are followed by the most frequently used common name(s). Plant size refers to the approximate height and width at maturity. Landscape use is described and may include suggestions for companion plants.

The hardiness ratings come from the United States Department of Agriculture Plant Hardiness Zone Map and indicate the northern and southern limits of each species. Following the hardiness ratings is the origin or native habitat of the species.

Important morphological features mentioned for each species include leaves, flowers, and (when ornamental) fruits. Most people think that the leaves of ground covers are their only ornamental feature. In reality, the leaves are usually just the beginning. Often the flowers and fruits display exceptional characteristics.

Growth rate indicates the relative rate of spread of each species, from slow to moderate, fast, and aggressive, while the spacing recommendation indicates how close plants can be sited. If plants are spaced as recommended and their cultural and care requirements are met, they will fill in completely in one to two growing seasons. Some of the slow-to-mature types, particularly the broad-spreading woody shrubs, may take up to four years to fill in.

Specific cultural recommendations regarding soil, moisture, and light requirements are given for each plant as are wind, humidity, pollution, or water table when appropriate. Maintenance requirements are noted as appropriate.

CONTENTS

Opposite: *Houttuynia cordata* 'Variegata'

PREFACE

Ground covers are materials used in landscaping expressly for the purpose of mulching or covering the soil. Wood chips, bark, the rinds or shells from fruits and nuts, stone, concrete, plastic, and turf grass are all ground covers. But this book is concerned with living, breathing ground covers, those vibrant plant species that oxygenate the air, control erosion, beautify our environment, and, when properly cultured and established, require little maintenance and densely cover the soil in a manner that discourages and prevents the growth of weeds. Although bamboos, ferns, ornamental grasses, rushes, and sedges can be used in the landscape as ground covers, they are not included in this pocket guide. Many tropicals also can be used as ground covers, but they too have been omitted because of space limitations within these pages.

For the most part, without pruning, ground covers range in height from less than 1 in. (2.5 cm) to about 4 ft. (1.2 m) tall. Ground covers may be woody, succulent, herbaceous, shrubby, or grasslike. They may be annual, biennial, or perennial. They can fall into the categories of clumping, vining, or sprawling, and they may be deciduous, evergreen, or semievergreen. Unlike turf grass and wood chips, which are plain green or boring brown, ground covers are available in an impressive array of colors and textures. In addition to green, they may be colored red, blue, purple, silver, coppery, bronze, or gold, and all shades in between. Variegated forms provide exciting combinations of colors and a wide range of textures from needle fine to coarse, feather soft to stiff and prickly. In keeping with our objective to minimize the work and maximize the fun of creating a landscape, this book discusses only perennial ground covers, those which live indefinitely.

Opposite: *Liriope muscari*

INTRODUCTION

Much annual cleanup work and expense can be eliminated by using ground covers under trees and shrubs instead of concrete, stone, or manicured turf. The ground covers break up the soil and discourage foot and lawn mower traffic, so the trees and shrubs benefit from better oxygen and water penetration, enhanced soil fertility, reduced soil compaction, and protection of their trunks from mechanical damage.

The financial advantages of ground covers are further reasons for using them. Generally, turf grass is less expensive to plant but more expensive to maintain with its need for frequent mowing, edging, fertilization, irrigation, disease and weed control, and leaf removal. Ground covers are also more practical than turf grass for facing buildings, trees, and shrubs simply because they eliminate the tiresome labor of mowing and trimming around and underneath them. Patios, courtyards, narrow strips paralleling walks and fences, areas under ornamental plants, and steep sloping hillsides can be extremely difficult to navigate with a lawn mower.

Ground covers exert numerous environmental benefits upon their immediate surroundings in addition to those related to the soil. They stabilize snow and reduce drifting during winter. Through transpiration (evaporative cooling) and photosynthesis, they cool and oxygenate the air during the warm season. Because they are typically green, they absorb light and reduce glare, an important factor making them useful in highway, roadside, and parking lot plantings. Furthermore, because ground covers are often deeply rooted and drought tolerant, they require less water than most turf grasses.

Ground Covers in the Landscape

In the landscape, ground covers can unify unrelated elements. For example, the striking contrast between a coarse-textured, vertically oriented, dark-colored house and a smooth-textured, horizontally oriented, light-colored (clear or blue) swimming pool can be lessened by surrounding the pool with a broad bed of blue-green mounding junipers.

Ground covers can soften the sharp edges and angles of boulders, benches, walkways, fences, stairs, buildings, and even other plants. Broad lush beds of ground covers near walkways and entryways communicate a pleasant, welcoming atmosphere to those who visit.

Additionally, ground covers can be used to alter our perception of space. Small-leaved, smooth-textured ground covers in wide, curving border plantings convey the impression of spaciousness, while larger-leaved, coarse-textured ground covers create a sense of intimacy. Shrubby ground covers with horizontal branching can be planted on steep slopes to make them seem more moderate. Brightly colored or fine-textured ground covers tend to brighten up areas and thereby elevate one's mood, while those in shades of blue, green, or gray tend to enhance feelings of tranquility and peacefulness.

Steps, entryways, decking, and shrubs are infinitely more interesting when accented with ground covers. With their intricate branch patterns, colorful foliage, and sometimes attractively flaking bark, ground covers relieve monotony in the landscape. Evergreen ground covers exhibit year-round beauty, while others grace us with flowers of heavenly scent and bright, beautiful color. All kinds of wildlife, including numerous songbirds, are attracted to their flowers and fruits—an added bonus to the environment and to the people who benefit from the entertainment these creatures provide.

Ground Covers for Facing Buildings

Ground covers employed to conceal the foundations of buildings are referred to as foundation

Opposite: *Tradescantia virginiana* 'Concord Grape'

Alchemilla mollis is often planted along shady wooded borders or as pathway edging, where its dew-covered pleated foliage can be fully appreciated by early-bird walkers.

plants. When planted close to buildings, standard shrubs and turf tend to look awkward or are functionally or physically inadequate (too short in the case of turf and too prone to damage or too cramped in the case of standard shrubs); however, many ground covers are ideally suited to such use.

The area closest to the base of a building can be an extremely difficult space in which to grow plants. Falling ice and heavy snow can be problems in cold climates, and reflected heat and torrents of rainwater can be troublesome in warmer ones and along the coasts. Here horizontally spreading ground covers are bothered little by the harshness of winter, are far more visually interesting than turf grass, bind soil during the most torrential dousing, and in many cases can withstand reflected light and heat.

In addition to causing erosion, rainwater may also cause less obvious damage as it falls from the roof. If left unchecked, the rain can form a gutter that channels water down to the subterranean foundation where it may saturate the surrounding soil, cause foundation damage, and eventually come into the basement. To help stabilize the soil and to prevent the formation of water channels, mat-forming, fibrous-rooted ground covers can be planted.

When planted around foundations, ground covers with succulent stems and leaves may act as fire breaks. Because they can help decrease the spread of flames, they are especially useful in hot, dry areas.

Combining Ground Covers with Bulbs, Spring Ephemerals, and Annuals

Bulbs and spring ephemerals supply interest and beauty in early spring, when still-dormant deciduous ground covers are leafless. Later, when the early blooming plants die back, the new ground cover growth blankets the soil that would normally remain exposed if the bulbs or ephemerals had been planted alone. Nice combinations are hostas and *Mertensia virginica* (Virginia bluebell), *Ceratostigma plumbaginoides* (dwarf plumbago), and crocuses or trilliums.

Annuals provide color throughout the growing season and combine nicely with low-growing, nonflowering ground covers. An attractive combination here is *Liriope muscari* 'Variegata' (variegated lily-turf) and yellow-flowered pansies. When interplanting with annuals, always pair the ground cover with an annual of complementary color and height, as well as cultural requirements.

Accent and Specimen Plantings

To emphasize or draw attention to particular features in the landscape, ground covers can be used as accent plants. Their bark, blossoms, foliage, and stems may accentuate the features of other plants, benches, entryways, ornaments, statues, steps, or garden structures. This contrast may be conveyed subtly, moderately, or boldly, depending on the choice of ground cover.

Distinctive ground covers can contribute unusual character and style when planted alone as specimens. The best locations are those to which the eye naturally falls, such as on hillsides and berms, or along banks that parallel ascending walks or steps. Planting in these areas will expose exceptional ground covers to the attention that they deserve, and they will make your landscape unique.

Ground Covers as Hedges

Ground covers may also be used for hedging. Obviously, they do not provide screening nor do they defend against invasion from the neighbor's pets and children, except in the case of a few thorny plants such as *Berberis* (barberry) and *Pyracantha* (firethorn). What they can help do, however, is identify property. By delimiting garden and border periphery, they may contribute to a garden style that is interesting, unusual, and esthetically pleasing.

Ceratostigma plumbaginoides softens the hard edges of a stone stairway.

Finding the Right Ground Cover

The process of finding the best ground cover for the job is very easy. It starts with determining your hardiness zone. The maps at the back of this book can help if you don't already know your zone.

Then assess the site you have selected. What is the condition of the soil—sandy or clay? Does it drain well or is it saturated? Is it acidic, alkaline, or neutral in pH? You can test the soil pH yourself with an inexpensive test kit or pH meter, available at most garden centers, or you can have the soil tested by your county horticultural extension agency.

Also check the light conditions of the site. For the sake of selecting ground covers, light conditions can be defined as follows:

Full sun: Locations exposed to direct, unshaded sunlight for at least six hours per day.

Light shade: Locations exposed to partially filtered sun, such as under open-canopied trees. Such sites receive a few hours of direct sun during some part of the day.

Moderate shade: Locations that receive more reflected light than direct sunlight, such as at the floor of a typical hardwood forest.

Heavy shade: Locations that receive almost no direct sunlight, such as at the base of a north-facing wall or below dense evergreens.

When you know your hardiness zone and the soil and light conditions of your planting site, determine the function you want your ground cover to perform. Using the lists of plants for specific purposes, identify suitable plants for your site and look up their descriptions. With that information, you can make an informed purchasing decision.

As you choose plants that will be hardy and that will perform the tasks assigned to them by you, keep in mind the three basic rules of designing with ground covers. First, use only one or a few selected varieties to avoid a cluttered appearance. Second, plant large-leaved ground covers when the scale is large and small-leaved ground covers when the scale is small. Third, combine only plants that will comfortably coexist—those with complementary cultural requirements, colors, textures, forms, and sizes—to avoid extra maintenance. Never combine a vigorous-growing, horizontally spreading species with one of diminutive or refined habit. The vigorous plant will completely overrun (and kill) the smaller, slower-growing one. Nearly as bad would be combining two fast-growing, horizontally spreading ground covers; the two would wage a constant struggle to take each other

Galium odoratum provides soft texture and mild fragrance in shady garden settings.

over, and the result would be a muddled, ugly appearance. Fast spreaders are usually best used alone, but two or more slow spreaders can often be combined effectively.

Planting Ground Covers

In cool climates you may plant successfully from spring through fall, and in hot or arid climates you may plant from fall through spring. Before planting, remove all existing turf grass, weeds, and debris. One way to accomplish this is to pin a sheet of black plastic on top of the site using rocks, bricks, or soil, a process that takes a couple of months and is best in sites with full sun. A second method is to spray the area with a systemic herbicide. The final method of weed control is old-fashioned but provides marvelous exercise. It involves repeatedly rototilling or spading the planting site until all vegetation has essentially been converted into soil through decomposers such as fungi, bacteria, and earthworms. Typically three or four turns of the site over five or six weeks will accomplish this objective.

After killing the weeds and loosening the soil, incorporate any amendments such as leaf mold, lime, organic compost, or topsoil with a spade or rototiller. For wide-spreading, woody, shrubby ground covers, only the area in the vicinity of the root zone needs to be amended. This is usually the top 8–12 in. (20–30 cm) of soil in an area about 3 ft. (90 cm) in diameter around the planting hole. The entire bed, however, must be amended for those plants that sprawl or spread by aboveground or underground horizontal stems, or have trailing branches, or are planted very close together. After you remove the weeds and add the amendments, complete the final grading with a rake.

Use a spade, trowel, or hoe to dig the necessary holes or trenches for planting. When setting plants into their holes, remember that the soil line at the base of the ground cover should be the same depth as it was in the container. Water the plants thoroughly, then top-dress the exposed soil between them with a layer of pine needles or wood chips about 2 in. (5 cm) thick.

Plants for ground cover need to be spaced evenly and at an appropriate distance apart so that plantings will be easy to maintain and will fill in at the same rate. Triangular spacing with plants staggered in parallel rows places all plants an equal distance apart. Square spacing places plants an equal distance from their neighbors above, below, or across, but not diagonally.

Maintaining Ground Covers

Probably the biggest advantage to using ground covers is that they require relatively little maintenance. However, like other plants, they may need occasional watering; weeding (until they become well established); pruning, thinning, and grooming; fertilizing; disease, insect, and rodent control; and in some cases, mowing.

Watering Ground Covers

Immediately after planting ground covers, water them in thoroughly until moisture penetrates a few inches (centimeters) deeper than the bottom of the roots. The roots of newly installed ground covers are small, and until they expand and become well established, frequent watering may be needed to prevent wilting. Three months is usually an adequate period for root establishment. From then on, water the plants only as needed.

Whenever possible, water shortly after sunrise so that the foliage can quickly dry, thus preventing fungal infection. Water only when necessary, evidenced by drying out of the soil or by a slight midday wilting of the leaves at the ends of the stems. Typically, little or no supplemental watering is necessary after the first year, except during extended hot, dry periods. In areas of freezing winter temperatures, water thoroughly in late fall, before the ground freezes solid, to enable plants to better cope with winter's harshness.

Controlling Weeds

The most critical step in weed control occurs before the plants are ever placed in the ground. Completely eliminating all weeds (including their roots) before you plant is essential to the rapid

Mazus reptans is dense and stays low, making it an effective filler between stepping stones.

Mulching helps to keep weed seeds from germinating and becoming established, and works just as well as preemergent herbicides. Simply resupply 1½–2 in. (4–5 cm) of wood chips, bark, or pine needles as the initial mulch thins and decomposes. In addition to not damaging the environment, organic mulches enrich the soil as they decompose.

Pruning Ground Covers

Although seldom necessary, many gardeners occasionally prune their ground covers to neaten them and to stimulate new growth and branching. The most useful tools for this task are hand shears, hedge shears, a string trimmer, or scissors. In some cases, a modified lawn mower is used.

Prune spring-flowering plants immediately after they bloom, summer- and fall-flowering plants in spring. Do not remove more than one-third of the length of the branches during a single pruning. Pruning more than that removes excessive leaf tissue and risks stressing the plants and predisposing them to disease and insect attack.

Fertilizing Ground Covers

Many ground covers benefit from one or two annual applications of organic or slow-release fertilizer. Low-grade soluble fertilizers are less expensive but can wash through the soil before the plant can use them completely. Because of this, they are more likely to contribute to groundwater contamination.

The ratio of nitrogen, phosphorus, and potassium in the fertilizer should be about 2–1–2. Such fertilizer can be applied first in early spring and then again in early fall. For a 10–5–10 formulation, apply at the rate of 1 lb. per 100 ft.² (450 g per 10 m²); for a 20–10–20 formulation, apply ½ lb. per 100 ft.² (227 g per 10 m²).

Dry fertilizer should only be applied when the leaves of the plants are dry; otherwise, the granules of fertilizer will adhere to the leaves and may spot or rot them. Following the application of fertilizer, immediately wash off (with a fast stream of water) any fertilizer that has adhered to or become trapped in the foliage.

establishment of ground covers. As the ground covers fill in, the need for weeding will taper off and eventually little or no weed control will be required. Until that time, ongoing weed control can be handled by manual hoeing or hand pulling, herbicides, or mulches.

Preemergent herbicides prevent weeds from becoming established but do not kill existing weeds. Postemergent herbicides kill weeds after they have come up. They must be used carefully as they may also kill your ground cover, if you happen to spray it.

Euonymus fortunei 'Coloratus' forms a dark green carpet that turns purplish in fall and winter.

Pachysandra terminalis thrives under oak trees and eliminates the need for raking up the leaves in fall.

Controlling Diseases and Pests

Like all plants, ground covers are susceptible to diseases and pests. This is why it is important to grow plants under ideal conditions, where they are at their most vigorous state and thus most resistant to diseases and pests. If frequent applications of chemicals become necessary to keep a ground cover healthy, chances are you have planted it in a location to which it is ill-suited.

Thinning Overcrowded Ground Covers

Sometimes ground covers grow together so tightly that they become overcrowded, resulting in stunted growth, reduced floral display, and increased susceptibility to disease. To correct overcrowding, uproot, separate, and reinstall the plants, leaving more space around individual plants. This process, known as thinning or dividing, is best accomplished during early spring to allow time for the plants to rebuild their root systems before the onslaught of summer.

Grooming Ground Covers

Leaves should only be raked up or vacuumed when they smother and mat down the ground cover. If fallen leaves slip through the ground cover canopy, allow them to remain there and decompose. This is what nature intended, and it will save you time and money. *Pachysandra terminalis* is an example of a ground cover that is coarse enough to absorb fallen oak leaves. The following spring the new growth obscures the oak leaves, which rot and furnish nutrients for the pachysandra.

When rainfall is infrequent or in polluted urban landscapes where the air contains much debris, dust can accumulate on the foliage of ground covers. Although dust may not be directly harmful, in time it reduces the amount of sunlight penetration and gas exchange (oxygen and carbon dioxide) and will stress and weaken your plants. This condition can be alleviated simply by washing the leaves with a fast stream of water, a practice that may also remove any aphids or mites from the plants.

Native Ground Covers

Although native plants are sometimes scorned as unattractive, untamed, too common, or too boring for landscape use, they grow in well-defined ecological niches and often are beautiful beyond description. Indeed, North American natives are among the showiest ground covers. Another reason to recommend natives is because they look right; they appear to be at home in our landscapes. Two outstanding North American natives are *Parthenocissus quinquefolia* (Virginia creeper), which yields attractive blue grapelike fruit that helps to feed numerous woodland creatures and birds, and *Arctostaphylos uva-ursi* (bearberry), among the most durable plants for full sun, strong winds, and pure sand.

Variegated Ground Covers

In a garden of subtly contrasting greens, a variegated selection commands attention, while its all-green parent might go unnoticed. Viewed from a distance, variegated ground covers convey an impression of color that is a blend of their component colors. Gold-edged cultivars will appear sunny from a distance, while masses of all-green forms impose a cool tranquility.

When using variegated ground covers, choose a color scheme and work with it. Plants with white variegation generally should not be located next to variegated plants of another color, but they combine wonderfully with green-foliaged plants—particularly those with pink, red, mauve, or purplish flowers—or with purple-, bronze-, coppery-, red-, or blue-leaved plants. Green-and-white-variegated plants enhance our perception of spaciousness and seem to function best in mass plantings on a moderate to large scale.

Plants with yellow or gold variegation lend themselves to specimen and accent planting—if used alone or in small groups. They also are excellent for edging borders, where moderate to high contrast is best.

Selections displaying three or more colors behave similarly to those of yellow-and-green variation. With its combination of green, yellowish, cream, and purple hues, *Houttuynia cordata* 'Variegata' appears maroon from a distance. At close range it looks quite busy, but it is this quality which enables this plant to command the attention of passersby.

Invasive Species

Some people believe that native plants perform better and support wildlife better in their local area. My perspective, with 23 years of experience as a grower and gardener of both native and nonnative plants, is that native plants are great in natural areas and in some landscape settings, but they are not inherently better adapted to home and commercial landscapes, nor do they necessarily furnish more or better food or habitat for wildlife. Landscape settings are not the same as natural settings—they are much brighter (due to light reflected from buildings), hotter (from sunlight being absorbed by brick and asphalt), higher in salt content (due to ice control and fertilization), full of disturbed or compacted soil with altered microflora and pH (from excavation activities), more polluted (from auto exhaust and mowers), and are often windier and drier than natural settings.

Because such landscapes are not native, plants that have evolved in the local natural environment don't always perform (or even survive) in them as well as plants from other geographic regions. Some of our most useful plants, like Japanese yew, certain dogwoods and viburnums, daylilies, and hostas, are not native, but they do a terrific job as landscape plants—without posing a threat to our native plant communities. As such they control erosion, beautify our constructed environments, furnish food, nectar, and nesting sites, cool and oxygenate the air, and produce organic matter which enriches the soil and perpetuates the cycle of life.

Several points must be understood to make sense of the invasive plant issue. First, one must

Hostas are beyond compare for returning so much beauty and usefulness for so little work.

account for geographical and climatological differences. For example, *Lonicera japonica* (Japanese honeysuckle vine) can grow 20 ft. (6 m) or more in a single year in the Midsouth (Tennessee, Kentucky, Carolinas, Georgia), where it produces copious seed which is dispersed (by birds) across spatial gaps (oftimes defined as 0.6 mi [1 km] or more) far away from its initial location. Here it clearly is an invasive plant. But, in Zones 4 to 6 of Michigan, where the growing season is too short for significant seed production and the species grows more slowly, *L. japonica* is quite easily contained.

A second factor to consider is the biology and history of the plant. It is illogical to assume that any nonnative plant in a natural area is invasive, as the plant may have gotten there by unnatural means. *Vinca minor* (common periwinkle), a dense grower that is able to outcompete less vigorous species, does not effectively reproduce from seed and therefore cannot disperse across spatial gaps. The reason it can sometimes be found in natural areas is that somebody planted it there. Usually this can be traced to its historical use as a grave site adornment, inappropriately dumped yard waste, or a landscape relic from a preexisting home site. Once eradicated, common periwinkle will not return to the natural area unless reintroduced by human intervention.

When talking about plants, one must avoid confusing the terms *invasive* and *assertive spreading*. One must consider the ability, speed, and quantity at which, by natural means, a plant can jump across spatial gaps away from the original population and reestablish, reproduce, and resist eradication. Truly invasive plants usually produce prodigious viable seed that can be transported to natural areas, while many assertive-spreading plants are easily contained.

Another thing one must do is to properly identify the plant in question. Many times this means avoiding the use of common names or the genus name by itself. When talking about purple loosestrife, for example, it is important to indicate *Lythrum salicaria*—for there are over 30 species of *Lythrum*, many with purple flowers, and not all of them are invasive. Some are native. Even if a species is determined to be invasive, one of its varieties or cultivars may not be invasive—due to sterility, dwarfism, or some other condition which generally limits its dispersal or reproductive effectiveness. Every plant must be evaluated individually.

A potentially invasive plant should only be sold with specific recommendations about its use. The label for *Lonicera japonica* should note that the species is invasive in Zones 7 to 10, where it grows fast and produces seed that is distributed by birds and wildlife, but in Zones 4 to 6, where it lacks sufficient time to produce much mature seed, it may be responsibly used in parts of landscapes that do not border natural areas.

Certainly some introduced plants have escaped from gardens and become invasive. Nursery managers should avoid future incidents by testing plants on a small scale and destroying those that demonstrate invasive qualities. It is through everyone's involvement that we can preserve our natural ecosystems as well as maximize the positive environmental and esthetic potential of all garden plants.

GROUND COVERS
FOR SPECIFIC PURPOSES AND LOCATIONS

The lists that follow are representative only and do not include every ground cover described in this guide.

Leaves Variegated Green and White

Euonymus fortunei 'Canadian Variegated'
Fallopia japonica 'Variegata'
Ficus pumila 'Variegata'
Hedera colchica 'Dentata Variegata'
Hedera helix 'Little Diamond'
Hosta 'Brim Cup'
Hosta 'Diamond Tiara'
Hosta 'Patriot'
Juniperus procumbens 'Variegata'
Thymus serpyllum 'Argenteus'
Trachelospermum jasminoides 'Variegatum'
Vinca minor 'Argenteo-variegata'

Leaves Variegated Green and Gold

Abelia ×*grandiflora* 'Francis Mason'
Euonymus fortunei 'Emerald 'n' Gold'
Euonymus fortunei 'Sparkle 'n' Gold'
Euonymus fortunei 'Sun Spot'
Hedera colchica 'Sulfur Heart'
Hedera helix 'California Gold'
Hedera helix 'Goldheart'
Hosta 'Gold Standard'
Hosta 'Golden Tiara'
Juniperus horizontalis 'Aurea'
Liriope muscari 'Gold Band'
Melissa officinalis 'Variegata'
Thymus serpyllum 'Aureus'
Vinca major 'Gold Vein'
Vinca minor 'Aureo-variegata'

Ground Covers Tolerant of Foot Traffic

Liriope spicata
Ophiopogon japonicus

Ground Covers Tolerant of Limited Foot Traffic

Acaena microphylla
Ajuga reptans
Arctostaphylos uva-ursi
Arctotheca calendula
Chamaemelum nobile
Chrysogonum virginianum
Duchesnea indica
Ficus pumila
Gaultheria procumbens
Gazania rigens
Herniaria glabra
Isotoma fluviatilis
Leptinella squalida
Lysimachia nummularia
Mazus reptans
Mentha requienii
Mitchella repens
Sagina subulata
Soleirolia soleirolii
Vinca spp.
Waldsteinia ternata

Ground Covers for Controlling Erosion

Abelia ×*grandiflora*
Acacia redolens
Aegopodium podagraria 'Variegatum'
Arctostaphylos uva-ursi
Arctotheca calendula
Baccharis pilularis
Carpobrotus edulis
Cephalophyllum alstonii
Ceratostigma plumbaginoides
Cistus salviifolius
Convallaria majalis
Coprosma ×*kirkii*
Coronilla varia

Opposite: *Salvia nemorosa* 'Caradonna'

Dampiera diversifolia
Drosanthemum floribundum
Duchesnea indica
Erica carnea
Euonymus fortunei
Gelsemium sempervirens
Geranium spp.
Grevillea juniperina
Hedera canariensis
Hypericum calycinum
Indigofera kirilowii
Iris spp.
Jasminum nudiflorum
Juniperus spp.
Lamiastrum galeobdolon
Lampranthus spectabilis
Lantana ×hybrida
Lotus corniculatus
Lysimachia clethroides
Myoporum parvifolium
Pachysandra terminalis
Parthenocissus quinquefolia
Pittosporum tobira 'Wheeler's Dwarf'
Rhus aromatica 'Grow-low'
Rubus calycinoides
Sedum reflexum
Stephanandra incisa 'Crispa'
Trachelospermum jasminoides
Vinca spp.

Fire-Retardant Ground Covers

Achillea millefolium
Aptenia cordifolia
Baccharis pilularis
Begonia grandis
Cephalophyllum alstonii
Crassula multicava
Delosperma spp.
Lampranthus spectabilis
Myoporum parvifolium
Osteospermum fruticosum
Sedum spp.

Salt-Tolerant Ground Covers

Acacia redolens
Arctostaphylos uva-ursi
Armeria maritima
Artemisia spp.
Aubrieta deltoidea
Aurinia saxatilis
Carissa macrocarpa
Cistus salviifolius
Coprosma ×kirkii
Dalea greggii
Erica carnea
Erigeron karvinskianus
Juniperus conferta
Juniperus horizontalis
Lonicera japonica
Muehlenbeckia axillaris
Parthenocissus quinquefolia

Drought-Tolerant Ground Covers

Abelia ×grandiflora
Acacia redolens
Achillea millefolium
Aptenia cordifolia
Arabis caucasica
Arctostaphylos uva-ursi
Arctotheca calendula
Armeria maritima
Artemisia spp.
Asparagus densiflorus 'Sprengeri'
Atriplex semibaccata
Baccharis pilularis
Berberis thunbergii 'Crimson Pygmy'
Callirhoe involucrata
Carpobrotus edulis
Cephalophyllum alstonii
Cerastium tomentosum
Chamaemelum nobile
Cistus salviifolius
Coprosma ×kirkii
Coreopsis verticillata
Coronilla varia
Crassula multicava
Cytisus decumbens
Dalea greggii
Drosanthemum floribundum

Duchesnea indica
Echeveria elegans
Erigeron karvinskianus
Euphorbia amygdaloides var. *robbiae*
Fallopia japonica 'Compacta'
Gardenia jasminoides 'Radicans'
Genista pilosa
Iberis sempervirens
Juniperus spp.
Lampranthus spectabilis
Lantana ×*hybrida*
Liriope spp.
Myoporum parvifolium
Nepeta ×*faassenii*
Osteospermum fruticosum
Penstemon pinifolius
Perovskia atriplicifolia
Polygonatum odoratum
Rhus aromatica 'Grow-low'
Rosmarinus officinalis
Sedum spp.
Xanthorhiza simplicissima
Zauschneria californica

Ground Covers for Wet (Saturated) Soil

Chelone lyonii
Coprosma ×*kirkii*
Lysimachia clethroides
Mentha requienii
Myosotis scorpioides
Persicaria filiformis
Petasites japonicus
Ranunculus repens

Ground Covers for Moderate to Dense Shade

Aegopodium podagraria 'Variegatum'
Asarum europaeum
Clivia miniata
Convallaria majalis
Cymbalaria spp.
Euonymus fortunei
Galium odoratum
Hedera spp.
Hosta spp.
Ligularia tussilaginea

Oxalis oregana
Pachysandra spp.
Polygonatum odoratum
Sarcococca hookeriana var. *humilis*
Saxifraga stolonifera
Soleirolia soleirolii
Tiarella wherryi
Vinca spp.
Xanthorhiza simplicissima

Ground Covers for Light to Moderate Shade

Abelia ×*grandiflora*
Acanthus mollis
Aegopodium podagraria 'Variegatum'
Ajuga reptans
Alchemilla mollis
Astilbe ×*arendsii*
Begonia grandis
Brunnera macrophylla
Carissa macrocarpa
Ceratostigma plumbaginoides
Chrysogonum virginianum
Cornus canadensis
Epimedium spp.
Francoa ramosa
Gardenia jasminoides 'Radicans'
Gaultheria spp.
Houttuynia cordata 'Variegata'
Iris cristata
Iris pseudacorus
Jasminum nudiflorum
Lamiastrum galeobdolon
Lamium maculatum
Liriope spp.
Lithodora diffusa
Lysimachia nummularia
Mazus reptans
Mitchella repens
Myosotis scorpioides
Nandina domestica
Parthenocissus quinquefolia
Persicaria filiformis
Petasites japonicus
Phlox divaricata
Ranunculus repens

Stylophorum diphyllum
Trachelospermum jasminoides
Viburnum davidii
Viola odorata
Waldsteinia ternata

Ground Covers for Light Shade

Acacia redolens
Aptenia cordifolia
Arabis caucasica
Asparagus densiflorus 'Sprengeri'
Atriplex semibaccata
Aubrieta deltoidea
Aurinia saxatilis
Berberis thunbergii 'Crimson Pygmy'
Bergenia cordifolia
Callirhoe involucrata
Calluna vulgaris
Campanula carpatica
Chamaemelum nobile
Chelone lyonii
Clematis maximowicziana
Coprosma ×kirkii
Coreopsis verticillata
Coronilla varia
Crassula multicava
Cuphea hyssopifolia
Dalea greggii
Dampiera diversifolia
Deutzia gracilis
Disporum sessile
Duchesnea indica
Echeveria elegans
Erica carnea
Euphorbia amygdaloides var. robbiae
Fallopia japonica 'Compacta'
Felicia amelloides
Gelsemium sempervirens
Genista pilosa
Geranium spp.
Herniaria glabra
Hypericum calycinum
Iberis sempervirens
Isotoma fluviatilis
Lantana ×hybrida
Lonicera japonica

Mentha requienii
Microbiota decussata
Phlox divaricata
Pittosporum tobira 'Wheeler's Dwarf'
Rhus aromatica 'Grow-low'
Rubus calycinoides
Sagina subulata
Stachys byzantina
Stephanandra incisa 'Crispa'

Ground Covers for Small Areas

Acaena microphylla
Aubrieta deltoidea
Cymbalaria spp.
Geranium cinereum
Isotoma fluviatilis
Lamium maculatum
Lithodora diffusa
Lysimachia nummularia
Mazus reptans
Melissa officinalis
Mentha requienii
Sagina subulata
Sempervivum spp.
Soleirolia soleirolii
Thymus serpyllum

Ground Covers for Large Areas

Baccharis pilularis
Carpobrotus edulis
Clematis maximowicziana
Coprosma ×kirkii
Coronilla varia
Gelsemium sempervirens
Indigofera kirilowii
Jasminum nudiflorum
Parthenocissus quinquefolia
Rhus aromatica 'Grow-low'

North American Native Ground Covers

Arctostaphylos uva-ursi
Artemisia stelleriana
Baccharis pilularis
Callirhoe involucrata
Chelone lyonii
Chrysogonum virginianum

Coreopsis verticillata
Cornus canadensis
Dalea greggii
Echevaria elegans
Gaultheria procumbens
Gaultheria shallon
Gelsemium sempervirens
Helleborus ×hybridus
Iris cristata
Juniperus horizontalis
Mahonia nervosa
Mahonia repens
Mitchella repens
Oxalis oregana
Pachysandra procumbens
Parthenocissus quinquefolia
Penstemon pinifolius
Phlox divaricata
Phlox subulata
Ranunculus repens
Rhus aromatica
Tiarella wherryi
Zauschneria californica

Ground Covers for Fall Bloom

Abelia ×grandiflora
Achillea millefolium
Asparagus densiflorus 'Sprengeri'
Begonia grandis
Calluna vulgaris
Ceratostigma plumbaginoides
Chelone lyonii
Clematis maximowicziana
Coronilla varia
Cymbalaria spp.
Drosanthemum floribundum
Erigeron karvinskianus
Fallopia japonica 'Compacta'
Felicia amelloides
Gardenia jasminoides 'Radicans'
Hypericum calycinum
Origanum laevigatum
Perovskia atriplicifolia
Persicaria affinis
Persicaria filiformis
Rudbeckia fulgida

Sarcococca hookeriana var. humilis
Stachys byzantina
Zauschneria californica

Ground Covers for Winter Bloom

Cephalophyllum alstonii
Clivia miniata
Crassula multicava
Echeveria elegans
Erica carnea
Erigeron karvinskianus
Grevillea juniperina
Lampranthus productus
Petasites japonicus
Sarcococca hookeriana var. humilis
Saxifraga stolonifera

Ground Covers for Spring Bloom

Acacia redolens
Ajuga spp.
Arctostaphylos uva-ursi
Asarum europaeum
Ceanothus spp.
Convallaria majalis
Dicentra spp.
Euphorbia amygdaloides var. robbiae
Galium odoratum
Iberis sempervirens
Pachysandra terminalis
Phlox spp.
Rosmarinus officinalis
Spiraea japonica
Vinca spp.
Viola spp.
Waldsteinia ternata
Xanthorhiza simplicissima

Ground Covers for Summer Bloom

Acaena microphylla
Acanthus mollis
Anagallis monellii
Armeria maritima
Artemisia spp.
Astilbe ×arendsii
Calamintha nepeta
Calluna vulgaris

Campanula carpatica
Cuphea hyssopifolia
Dampiera diversifolia
Felicia amelloides
Francoa ramosa
Gazania rigens
Genista pilosa
Geranium spp.
Herniaria glabra
Ilex crenata
Indigofera kirilowii
Iris ensata
Iris pseudacorus
Lavandula angustifolia
Ligularia tussilaginea
Liriope spp.
Lithodora diffusa

Lonicera japonica
Lotus corniculatus
Myosotis scorpioides
Nandina domestica
Nepeta ×faassenii
Pernettya mucronata
Perovskia atriplicifolia
Persicaria filiformis
Ranunculus repens
Rubus calycinoides
Rudbeckia fulgida
Saxifraga stolonifera
Stachys byzantina
Stephanandra incisa 'Crispa'
Stylophorum diphyllum
Viburnum davidii
Zauschneria californica

Opposite: *Disporulm sessile* 'Variegatum'

Abelia ×grandiflora
Glossy abelia

Dense and rounded, glossy abelia provides a long and engaging floral show. It is useful for mass planting on a large scale and, because it binds the soil well, is prized on steep slopes and freeway embankments. Zones 6–9.

A semievergreen, many-stemmed shrub 3–6 ft. (90–180 cm) tall and wide. Leaves simple, oval, ½–1¼ in. (12–30 mm) long, edges toothed, lustrous dark green above and paler green below, bronzy in fall and winter, on reddish brown stems. Flowers funnel shaped, ¾ in. (2 cm) long and wide, pale pink to white, aging to purple, mid summer to early fall.

Slow growing; space 30–48 in. (75–120 cm) apart. Well-drained, acidic, rich loam. Moderately drought tolerant. Light to moderate shade. Prune annually to remove dead stems.

'Francis Mason', leaves variegated yellow and green.

'Prostrata', only 18–24 in. (45–60 cm) tall.

'Sherwoodii', juvenile leaves reddish and, like the flowers, smaller than the species.

Abelia ×grandiflora

Acacia redolens

Acacia redolens
Trailing acacia, sweet wattle

Trailing acacia is one of the best ground covers for highly saline, arid soils in deserts, where it performs well both for erosion control and as a turf replacement in moderate to large, level or sloping areas. Zones 9–10. Australia.

A low, shrub 1–4 ft. (30–120 cm) tall by 10–15 ft. (3.0–4.5 m) wide. Leaves narrow, evergreen, 3½ in. (9 cm) long by ½ in. (2 cm) wide, subtle gray-green. Flowers dainty, ball shaped, yellow, ⅛ in. (3 mm) in diameter, spring. Fruit a tiny pod.

Fast growing; space 4–6 ft. (1.2–1.8 m) apart. Well-drained, acidic, sandy and rocky soils. Very drought tolerant after the first season. Full sun.

Shear periodically to maintain a neat, compact appearance.

Acaena microphylla
Redspine sheepburr

Redspine sheepburr is best used on a small scale as a general cover or as a filler between stepping stones. Zones 6–9. New Zealand.

A low-growing, mat-forming herb 4–6 in. (10–15 cm) tall and spreading indefinitely. Leaves 1 in. (2.5 cm) long, divided into 7 to 15 leaflets, and edged with rounded teeth, purplish to olive or bronzy green, with a soft fine texture. Flowers grayish, insignificant. Fruit bristly, crimson when ripe, lends interest in summer.

Acaena microphylla

Acaena microphylla
Copper Carpet

Acanthus mollis

Fast growing; space 10–16 in. (25–40 cm) apart. Sandy, well-drained, alkaline, moist or dry soils. Very drought tolerant. Full sun.

Copper Carpet (syn. 'Kupferteppich'), red-brown foliage.

Acanthus mollis
Bear's breech, artist's acanthus

Bear's breech is often used as a specimen or background plant in perennial borders. On a larger scale it functions as a foundation facer or edging plant. Zones 6–10. Mediterranean area.

A stemless, clump-forming herb 2–3 ft. (60–90 cm) tall and 6 ft. (1.8 m) wide. Leaves large, arising from the crown, dark glossy green, lobed, deeply cut, evergreen, oblong to oval, 18–24 in. (45–60 cm) long by 12 in. (30 cm) wide, with conspicuous veins. Flowers white to pinkish, in erect spikes 12–18 in. (30–45 cm) long, late spring to early summer.

Moderate to fast growing; space 30–42 in. (75–105 cm) apart. Slightly moist, rich, well-drained, acidic soil. Light to moderate shade. Remove the flower stalks after blooming and trim out tattered leaves as they occur.

'Hollard's Gold', golden leaves

Latifolius Group, broader leaves, greater cold tolerance.

'Oak Leaf', leaves shaped like oak leaves.

'Summer Dream', possibly a hybrid between *A. mollis* and *A. spinosus*, numerous white tubular flowers with pinkish purple bracts.

Achillea millefolium
Milfoil, common yarrow

Milfoil remains popular because its flowers and fernlike foliage add color, texture, and fragrance to the landscape. It also attracts beneficial insects, including ladybugs and butterflies. Sometimes self-sowing, it is suitable for small to moderate, casual, wild, chaotic, or contained areas where it may spread freely. It is also used as a companion plant in the herbaceous border or rock garden. Zones 3–10. Europe; widely naturalized in temperate regions.

Achillea millefolium 'Ortel's Rose'

Achillea millefolium 'Red Beauty'

An erect to sprawling herb, 3 ft. (90 cm) tall, spreading indefinitely. Leaves fine-textured, nearly evergreen, 8 in. (20 cm) long, aromatic, medium green, divided two or three times. Flowers tiny, whitish, in flat-topped clusters 2 to 3 in. (5.0–7.5 cm) wide, mid summer to mid autumn.

Fast growing; space 8–16 in. (20–40 cm) apart. Infertile, well-drained sandy loam. Very drought tolerant. Full sun. Cut flowers back in summer to extend blooming season. Remove flowers as they fade to prevent self-sowing. Divide crowded clumps every two to four years.

'Cerise Queen', bright cherry red flowers.
'Fire King', rose-red flowers, silvery foliage.
'Kelwayi', magenta-red flowers.
'Lilac Beauty', soft lilac flowers.
'Ortel's Rose', soft pastel pink flowers.
'Paprika', red flowers.
'Red Beauty', red flowers.
'Red Velvet', deep red flowers.
'Roseum', pink flowers, silvery green foliage.
'White Beauty', large clusters of pure white flowers.

Aegopodium podagraria
Bishop's weed, goutweed

This potentially weedy herb has foliage resembling that of an ash or elder tree and nonshowy flowers resembling its relative, Queen Anne's lace. It is well suited for covering moderate to large areas where its rootstock can be kept in check. It thrives in a woodland border in the shade of large deciduous trees and promotes a sense of continuity between the woodland and the artificial features of the landscape. It is excellent also for sites between building foundations and sidewalks, where its spread is contained. Zones 3–9. Europe.

A rhizomatous herb 6–14 in. (15–35 cm) tall, spreading indefinitely. Leaves deciduous, medium green, carrot-scented, divided into three leaflets that are each further divided into three subleaflets 1 1/2–3 in. (4.0–7.5 cm) long by 1 1/2 in. (4 cm) wide. Flowers small, whitish, in clusters, on stems 1–2 ft. (30–60 cm) tall, summer.

Very fast growing, except in drought or infertile soil; space 10–14 in. (25–35 cm) apart. Any soil,

Aegopodium podagraria 'Variegatum'

including compacted and infertile soils. Drought tolerant, yet often wilts midday when soil moisture becomes depleted. Full sun to dense shade.

'Variegatum', more commonly grown than the species; foliage with silvery white and green variegation, excellent for brightening areas in deep shade.

Agapanthus praecox subsp. orientalis
Oriental agapanthus

When mass planted, Oriental agapanthus is outstanding both for magnificent flowers and for graceful, soft-textured, arching foliage. It is excellent for edging borders and, when planted in groups, as an accent. The flowers are attractive to hummingbirds. Zones 9–11. South Africa.

A robust, lilylike, clump-forming herb 20–35 in. (50–90 cm) tall. Leaves evergreen, to 2 ft. (60 cm) long by 2 in. (5 cm) wide, dark glossy green. Flowers blue, funnel shaped, 2 in. long, in clusters of 40 to 110, on stalks 4–6 ft. (1.2–1.8 m) tall, mid spring to early fall.

Moderate growing; space 18–24 in. (45–60 cm) apart. Sandy, well-aerated soil best with constant but low moisture; well-drained heavier soils tolerated. Full sun to partial shade. Cut off flower stalks each fall after blooming. Divide crowded plants every five to six years.

'Variegatus', leaves striped white and green.

Agapanthus hybrids
Love flower hybrids

Like so many other popular florific groups, agapanthuses have been hybridized extensively and the parentage of popular cultivars isn't well documented. Those listed here are likely of hybrid origin.

'Back in Black', jet black stems, dark purple-blue flowers.

'Blue Giant', large deep blue flowers.

'Blue Triumphator', giant azure flowers.

'Bressingham Blue', deep amethyst-blue flowers.

'Bressingham White', tall, large white flowers.

'Giganteus', sturdy spikes with clusters of about 200 dark blue flowers.

Agapanthus praecox subsp. *orientalis* 'Variegatus'

Headbourne Hybrids, mid blue flowers, cold hardy to Zone 5 or 6.

'Lilliput', 18 in. (45 cm) tall, light blue flowers.

'Loch Hope', 4–5 ft. (1.2–1.5 m) tall, deep violet flowers, late blooming.

'Midnight Star', deep blue flowers.

'Mooreanus', dark blue flowers, possibly cold hardy to Zone 8.

'Peter Pan', only 12 in. (30 cm) tall, deep blue flowers.

'Sea Foam', only 12 in. (30 cm) tall, white flowers in clusters 4 in. (10 cm) wide.

'Snowy Owl', creamy white flowers.

'Tinkerbell', only 12 in. (30 cm) tall, violet-blue flowers, green foliage edged with white.

AJUGA
Bugleweed

Bugleweeds are popular for their ability to spread quickly, along with their burst of springtime floral color and the rich bronzy foliage of many of the cultivars. They are used on a small to moderate scale as a substitute for turf grass or as a facing plant to sedums, candytuft, hostas, ferns, and broad-spreading shrubs. They are also planted underneath deep-rooted trees. Bumblebees and hummingbirds love their flowers.

Agapanthus 'Midnight Star'

Ajuga reptans 'Bronze Beauty', flowers

Fast growing; space 14 in. (35 cm) apart. Moist but well-drained, sandy, acidic loam. Shelter from strong winds. Full sun only along the coast; light to moderate shade elsewhere. Trim back plants as they outgrow their bounds. Mow flowers as they begin to fade.

Ajuga reptans
Creeping bugleweed

A low-growing herb 3–4 in. (7.5–10.0 cm) tall, spreading indefinitely. Leaves glossy, medium green, oval, 3–4 in. (7.5–10.0 cm) long, semievergreen to evergreen, in tight rosettes. Flowers long-lasting, vibrant, highly visible, bluish violet, vaguely fragrant, in masses, late spring. Zones 3–9. Central Europe.

'Alba', creamy white flowers.

'Brocade', large silvery purple leaves, blue flowers.

'Bronze Beauty', purplish bronze leaves.

'Burgundy Glow', burgundy, pink, creamy white, and green leaves.

'Catlin's Giant', robust habit, huge metallic bronzy leaves, bluish flowers.

'Gaiety' (syn. 'Bronze Improved'), robust habit, bronzy purple leaves.

'Mahogany', deep, dark purple foliage, blue flowers.

Ajuga reptans
'Bronze Beauty', foliage

Ajuga reptans
'Catlin's Giant'

Ajuga reptans 'Purple Torch'

Ajuga tenorii 'Chocolate Chip'

'**Mini Crispa Red**', miniature form with wrinkled, bronze leaves.

'**Pink Elf**', compact form, bronze leaves, pink flowers.

'**Purple Torch**', lavender flowers, bronze leaves.

'**Rosea**', rose-pink flowers.

'**Royalty**', dark purple leaves.

'**Silver Beauty**', gray-green leaves with silvery white edges.

'**Thumbelina**', tiny shiny green leaves.

Ajuga tenorii

A very dense, rhizomatous perennial 2.5 in. (5 cm) tall, spreading indefinitely. Leaves (12 cm) long, oblong to spatula shaped, edged with teeth. Flowers bright blue, lacy, in spikes, spring to early summer. Zones 3–9. Italy, Sicily.

'**Chocolate Chip**', petite chocolate-colored leaves.

'**Emerald Chip**', green leaves.

Alchemilla mollis
Lady's mantle

Often lady's mantle is used on a small to moderate scale along shady wooded borders or as pathway edging. It combines well with pines, rhododendrons, azaleas, ferns, hostas, and astilbes. Zones 3–7. Europe.

A clump-forming herb 6–12 in. (15–30 cm) tall, gradually spreading to 2 ft. (60 cm) wide. Leaves attractively pleated, evergreen, rounded, 2–4 in. (5–10 cm) wide, hairy, gray-green, soft-textured. Flowers numerous, yellowish green, above the leaves, mid to late spring.

Slow growing; space 6–10 in. (15–25 cm) apart. Moist but well-drained, rich, neutral to slightly acidic loam. Full sun to moderate shade. Mow in late winter to keep plantings neat. Remove flowers shortly after they fade if reseeding is a problem.

'**Auslese**', pale yellow flowers.

Alchemilla mollis

Anagallis monellii
(photo by Pamela Harper)

Aptenia cordifolia
'Red Apple'

Arabis caucasica
Snow Cap (courtesy
of Walters Gardens)

Anagallis monellii
Monell's pimpernel, blue pimpernel

Valued for its prolonged display of colorful flowers, Monell's pimpernel makes an excellent specimen for the rock garden or perennial border. It can also be used on a small to moderate scale as a turf substitute. For level or sloping terrain, in an elevated planter, next to a retaining wall, or in a terrace, the cascading branches are very eye-catching. Zones 7–10. Mediterranean region.

A low-growing, sprawling, mounding herb 12–18 in. (30–45 cm) tall, spreading over 3 ft. (90 cm) wide. Leaves deciduous, oval to oblong, 1 in. (2.5 cm) long, dark green with reddish veins. Flowers solitary, 1/4–1 in. (6–25 mm) in diameter, gentian blue above, reddish below, summer.

Moderate to fast growing; space 2–3 ft. (60–90 cm) apart. Any well-drained, slightly moist soil. Tolerates short periods of drought. Full sun. Trim in late fall or early spring to keep plants compact and neat looking.

'Pacific Blue', more compact, 8–10 in. (20–25 cm) tall.

'Phillipii', deep gentian blue flowers.

'Skylover', larger, deeper blue flowers.

Aptenia cordifolia
Baby sun rose

This glossy leaved ground cover is suitable for small to large areas and is excellent in planters and rock gardens. Zones 9–11. South Africa.

A florific, creeping, succulent subshrub spreading over 4 ft. (1.2 m) wide. Leaves green, 1 in. (2.5 cm) long by 3/4 in. (2 cm) wide, oval to heart shaped, covered with water-soaked pimplelike projections. Flowers purple to red, on short stalks, spring and summer.

Moderate to fast growing; space 8–14 in. (20–35 cm) apart. Any acidic or neutral well-drained soil. Water established plants during prolonged periods of heat and drought. Moderately salt tolerant. Full sun to light shade.

'Alba', white flowers.

'Crystal', deep rose-colored flowers, green leaves with creamy white variegation.

'Red Apple', cheery orangish apple-red flowers.

'Variegata', leaves with white edges.

Arabis caucasica
Wall rock cress

Outstanding for its unusual leaf texture and pleasant flowers, wall rock cress is a very useful, small-scale soil stabilizer for rocky slopes. Between large stones in a rock garden or atop a retaining wall, it performs admirably as a specimen or accent plant. It combines well with candytuft, showy sedum, pygmy barberry, and blue fescue. Zones 4–10. Caucasus Mountains.

A somewhat tufted, somewhat trailing herb 6–12 in. (15–30 cm) tall, spreading 18 in. (45 cm) wide. Leaves semievergreen, oval with a long, tapering base, grayish green, 1–2 in. (2.5–5.0 cm) long, covered with tiny hairs, slightly lobed or coarsely toothed on the edges toward the leaf tips. Flowers white, fragrant, 3/8–5/8 in. (9–15 mm) wide, early to mid spring.

Moderate growing; space 8–12 in. (20–30 cm) apart. Sandy, well-drained, slightly acidic to alkaline soil. Water established plants occasionally in summer as needed. Full sun to light shade. Mow after flowering to keep plantings neat and compact.

'Floreplena', striking, double white flowers.

'Pinkie', intensely pink flowers.

'Rosabella', pink flowers aging to near white.

Snow Cap (syn. 'Schneehaube'), pure white flowers.

'Snow Peak', only 4 in. (10 cm) tall, single white flowers.

'Spring Charm', large clear pink flowers.

'Variegata', leaves with conspicuous creamy white irregular patches, often reverting to all green.

Arctostaphylos uva-ursi
Bearberry, kinnikinick

Common bearberry is an excellent ground cover in moderate to large informal and native-plant landscapes. It combines well with magnolias, high- and low-bush blueberries, witch hazels, dogwoods, pines, oaks, and serviceberries. Bearberry thrives in rugged conditions such as the sand or gravel of lakeshores and, even in the face of prevailing winds, it blankets steep slopes and controls erosion as few others. Zones 3–7. North America, Europe, Asia.

Arctostaphylos uva-ursi

A prostrate, low-growing, woody, creeping shrub 1–4 in. (2.5–10.0 cm) tall, spreading indefinitely. Leaves attractive, dark green, leathery, evergreen, teardrop shaped, 1 in. (2.5 cm) long, turning bronzy or reddish in fall and winter, becoming green in early to mid spring. Flowers numerous, miniature, urnlike, white to pinkish, spring. Fruit abundant, berrylike, 1/4–1/2 in. (6–12 mm) in diameter, green in late summer, red in autumn.

Slow to moderate growing; space 12–24 in. (30–60 cm) apart. Well-drained, sandy or gritty, acidic soil. Very drought resistant. Full sun to light shade but best in exposed, open sites with good air movement.

'Alaska', very low growing, small dark green, rounded leaves.

'Big Bear', vigorous growing, larger leaves.

'Emerald Carpet', more shade tolerant than the species, 10–18 in. (25–45 cm) tall by 6 ft. (1.8 m), leaves densely set and dark green.

'Massachusetts', shorter and more compact than the species, with more flowers and fruit.

Var. *microphylla*, leaves much smaller than the species.

'Pacific Mist', fast growing, grayish green leaves.

'Point Reyes', more heat and drought tolerant, with leaves darker green and more closely spaced.

'Radiant', leaves light green and widely spaced, fruiting heavily.

'Vancouver Jade', more vigorous, with flowers on semiupright branches and thus more visible.

Arctostaphylos uva-ursi, fruit

Arctostaphylos uva-ursi 'Massachusetts'

'Vulcan's Peak', more prolific in flowers and fruit.

'Wood's Compacta', 2–3 in. (5.0–7.5 cm) tall by 3–4 ft. (90–120 cm) wide, leaves small and green, tips turning red in fall, flowers white with pink tinge.

Arctotheca calendula
Cape weed, Cape dandelion

This tough, relatively aggressively spreading ground cover is sometimes a bit ragged appearing. It is best used for erosion control on slopes and as a general cover in large areas where sidewalks or curbs check its spread. It is particularly attractive and useful when allowed to trail over the edge of a stone retaining wall. Zones 9–11. South Africa.

A low-sprawling, leafy, carpeting herb 8–12 in. (20–30 cm) tall, spreading indefinitely. Leaves evergreen, coarse-textured, oblong to lyre shaped, gray-green, hairy, 6–8 in. (15–20 cm) long, 2 in. (5 cm) wide, deeply and irregularly furrowed about the edge. Flowers cheerful, solitary, daisylike, yellow, 1–2 in. (2.5–5.0 cm) wide, abundant in spring, sporadically the rest of the year.

Fast growing; space 14–20 in. (35–50 cm) apart. Any well-drained, slightly moist soil. Heat and drought tolerant. Full sun. Mow after flowering to thicken plantings and keep them neat.

Armeria maritima
Maritime thrift, common thrift

Common thrift is magnificently showy during its extended flowering season and has lovely dark green, grassy foliage year-round. It is best on a small to moderate scale where it provides excellent contrast and color when interplanted with other tufted ground covers. It performs well as a facing to open trees and erect or vase-shaped blue-leaved junipers. Single plants or small groups of thrift are splendid as specimens or accent plants in mixed herbaceous borders or island groupings. For artistic gardeners, thrift holds its shape well and can be arranged in geometric patterns. It is relatively tolerant of salt, making it a good choice for coastal gardens. Zones 4–8. Southern Greenland, Iceland, northwestern Europe.

Arctotheca calendula

Armeria maritima 'Brilliant'

Armeria maritima 'Dusseldorf Pride'

Armeria maritima 'Rubrifolia'

A low-growing, tuft-forming herb 4–6 in. (10–15 cm) tall, spreading 8–12 in. (20–30 cm) wide. Leaves thin, dark green to grayish, evergreen, 4 in. (10 cm) long. Flowers purple to white, round, in balloonlike heads, on thin green stalks, mid spring.

Slow growing; space 6–10 in. (15–25 cm) apart. Light, sandy loam with good drainage. Water only during extended periods of drought. Full sun to light shade; in hot climates, protect from afternoon sun. Divide crowded plants when they become brown in the center.

'Alba', white flowers.

'Bees Ruby', compact habit, with large, deep pink flowers.

'Brilliant', bright pink flowers.

'Cotton Tail', pure white flowers.

'Dusseldorf Pride', reddish to deep pinkish red flowers.

'Joy Stick', many pink flowers.

'Laucheana', deep crimson flowers.

'Nifty Thrifty', pink flowers, leaves with creamy variegation.

'Purpurea', purple flowers.

'Robusta', vigorous, with flower stalks to 15 in. (38 cm) tall.

Var. *rubra*, light red flowers, stalks 6–8 in. (15–20 cm) tall.

'Rubrifolia', rose-pink flowers, deep purplish red foliage.

'Ruby Glow', ruby red flowers, stalks 10 in. (25 cm) tall.

'Splendens', bright red flowers.

'Vindictive', deep rose-red flowers.

ARTEMISIA
Wormwood

The expansive genus *Artemisia* consists of about 200 species. The low-growing herbaceous or semi-woody perennials among them generally work well for covering small plots, as specimens in rock gardens, or for accent or edging in border settings. They are noteworthy primarily for their foliage.

Poor, infertile, relatively dry, acidic to neutral soils. Provide supplemental water only during prolonged drought. Full sun to light shade. Cut back ragged or tattered plantings to neaten them and to stimulate fresh growth.

Artemisia ludoviciana 'Valerie Finnis'

Artemisia stelleriana
'Silver Brocade' (courtesy
of Monrovia Nursery)

Asarum europaeum

Asarum splendens
'Quick Silver'

Artemisia ludoviciana
White sage, western mugwort
Suitable for prairies and dry sandy sites. A variable, durable herb 1–4 ft. (30–120 cm) tall, spreading 2–3 ft. (60–90 cm) wide. Leaves deciduous, silvery gray. Flowers tiny, gray, late summer. Zones 4–10. Michigan to British Columbia, south to Arkansas and Mexico.

'Latiloba', shorter than the species, with gray-green leaves 3 in. (7.5 cm) wide.

'Valerie Finnis', mat-forming, silvery blue-green foliage, especially nice when trailing over the edge of a boulder or retaining wall.

Artemisia stelleriana
Beach wormwood, dusty miller
Popular in seaside plantings because of its relatively high tolerance to salt. A herbaceous, shrubby plant 24–30 in. (60–75 cm) tall, spreading to 3 ft. (90 cm) wide. Leaves oblong to oval, woolly, white, 4 in. (10 cm) long. Flowers yellow, 1/4 in. (6 mm) in diameter, summer. Zones 3–9. Eastern North America.

Moderate growing; space 18–24 in. (45–60 cm) apart.

'Silver Brocade', 6–12 in. (15–30 cm) tall, more than 12 in. (30 cm) wide, very attractive, lacy, silvery white foliage on arching stems, few flowers.

ASARUM
Ginger
If it were not for their slow growth (and concomitant high price), gingers would be commonplace in nearly every tree-shaded landscape of North America. They are excellent for covering the woodland floor, display extremely handsome foliage, and require no maintenance. They look beautiful in small or large groups in woodland borders and underneath dense shade trees. Gingers combine well with trilliums, columbines, bellflowers, bleeding hearts, bunchberry, heucheras, and astilbes. They add contrast when interplanted with taller, clump-forming hostas (particularly blue forms) and cultivars of *Pulmonaria*.

Slow growing; space 8–12 in. (20–30 cm) apart. Constantly moist, rich, acidic soil. Shelter from strong winds. Light to dense shade in cool climates; moderate to dense shade in warm climates.

Asarum europaeum
European wild ginger
A dense, low-growing, horizontally spreading, leafy herb 5 in. (13 cm) tall by 14 in. (35 cm) wide. Leaves evergreen, leathery, dark glossy green, heart- to kidney shaped, 3 in. (7.6 cm) wide, often obscuring both flowers and fruit. Flowers greenish to purple or brown, 1/2 in. (12 mm) wide, spring. Zones 4–8. Europe.

Asarum splendens
A vigorous-spreading, rhizomatous herb 6 in. (15 cm) tall. Leaves dark green with gray mottling. Zones 5–9. Asia.

'Quick Silver', larger leaves with silvery veining.

Asparagus densiflorus
Asparagus fern
In the United States, asparagus fern is frequently planted along the southern coasts and in the Deep South but in northern climates is known as a florist's plant, common to cemetery urns and flower arrangements. As a ground cover, it excels in small to medium areas and often is used in raised beds and atop retaining walls and sea walls, over which its vibrant green sprays of foliage can gracefully cascade. Because it tends to climb upon other plants, it should be used only by itself or underneath open-canopied trees and tall shrubs. It tolerates airborne salt and is hence useful along the coasts. Zones 8–11. South Africa.

A tuberous, shrubby, horizontally spreading, vinelike ground cover 2–3 ft. (60–90 cm) tall and wide when unsupported. Leaves unusual, flattish, needlelike, 3/8–1 1/4 in. (9–30 mm) long, light green. Flowers mildly scented, insignificant, summer through fall. Fruit a small green berry, red in winter.

Slow to moderate growing; space 30–42 in. (45–75 cm) apart. Well-drained, neutral to slightly

Asparagus densiflorus 'Myers'

Asparagus densiflorus 'Sprengeri'

acidic loam. Water during extended dry periods. Full sun to light shade. Clip back plants as they outgrow their bounds or become ragged looking.

'Myers', Myer's asparagus fern, upright foliage reminiscent of a green luffa, pinkish white flowers. Fantastic for lining walkways.

'Sprengeri', Sprenger asparagus, large cushions of long, arching stems densely covered with dark green, needlelike leaves.

'Sprengeri Compactus', shorter and less open in habit.

'Sprengeri Deflexus', foliage has a metallic sheen.

'Sprengeri Robustus', more vigorous habit.

Astilbe ×arendsii
Astilbe, false spirea

False spirea is among the most easily cultivated, most colorful, most durable, and most forgiving of ground covers. Alone or with ferns, hostas, irises, bergenias, sedges, and many clump-forming ornamental grasses, it may be used on a small to large scale and is splendid as a coarse-textured colorful turf substitute. In small groups it can be used as a facing to statuary, boulders, shrubs, and small trees. A broad facing of astilbes can literally transform an ordinary fence into a landscape spectacle and, when used in masses around a doorway, the vibrant flowers and crisp foliage extend a cheerful greeting to visitors. Astilbes can also be used to line garden paths, soften pool edges, and enhance stream banks. Zones 4–9. Several species are involved in the parentage of hybrid astilbes.

An imposing herbaceous perennial 24–42 in. (60–105 cm) tall, spreading 2–3 ft. (60–90 cm) wide. Leaves compound, dark green to bronzy, leaflets oval to oblong with double-toothed edges. Flowers tiny, numerous, colored white, pink, purple, rose, or salmon, in erect clusters, summer.

Slow to moderate growing; space 15–18 in. (38–45 cm) apart. Constantly moist but well-drained, rich, acidic soil. Cool temperatures best. Light to moderate shade; full sun in alpine and coastal areas.

'Cattleya', light pink flowers.

'Erica', clear pink flowers.

'Fanal', dark red flowers.

'Federsee', carmine-rose flowers.

Glow (syn. 'Glut'), bright red flowers, compact habit.

'Granat', carmine-red flowers.

'Irrlicht', rosy white flowers, dark green leaves.

'Spinell', salmon-red flowers.

White Gloria (syn. 'Weisse Gloria'), early blooming, white flowers.

Astilbe Glow

Astilbe White Gloria

Astilbe chinensis 'Visions'

Atriplex semibaccata
(photo by Richard Shiell)

Aurinia saxatilis
'Sulphureum'

Aubrieta deltoidea (courtesy of Walters Gardens)

Astilbe chinensis
Chinese astilbe

A tough perennial 8–12 in. (20–25 cm) tall and wide. Leaves divided into two or three oval leaflets, each 2–3½ in. (5–9 cm) long, hairy, tooth-edged. Flowers tiny, rose colored, on stout stalks above the foliage, mid to late summer. China.

'Finale', pale-mauve upright plumes.

'Pumila', purple-pink plumes to 12 in. (25 cm) tall, foliage short and compact.

'Superba', magenta pink plumes 3 ft. (90 cm) tall.

'Visions', dense rosy purple plumes to 1½ ft. (45 cm) tall.

Atriplex semibaccata
Creeping saltbush, Australian saltbush

Creeping saltbush is primarily planted in desert areas of the U.S. Southwest. Because it is relatively fire resistant, it is recommended as a facing plant for commercial buildings, homes, and parks. Its chief ornamental attribute is its foliage. Zones 8–10. Australia.

A mounding, horizontally spreading, mat-forming, deep-rooted, woody ground cover 12–18 in. (30–45 cm) tall, spreading over 6 ft. (1.8 m) wide. Leaves gray, evergreen, fine-textured, densely set, 1–1½ in. (2.5–4.0 cm) long, edges unevenly toothed.

Fast growing; space 42–54 in. (105–135 cm) apart. Infertile, saline, sandy, well-drained soils. Drought tolerant, but give an occasional deep watering during the summer. Full sun to light shade.

'Corto', 10 in. (25 cm) tall, gray-green foliage.

Aubrieta deltoidea
Purple rock cress, false rock cress

Attractive for its handsome foliage and flowers, purple rock cress is best planted between large stones in rock gardens or allowed to trail over a retaining wall. As a small-scale general cover or a foreground plant, it combines nicely with candytuft, phlox, alyssum, and other perennials of contrasting floral color. Zones 4–8. Greece.

A matlike, horizontally spreading, slightly mound-forming, rhizomatous herb 3–6 in. (7.5–15.0 cm) tall, spreading 12–18 in. (30–45 cm) wide. Leaves evergreen, grayish green, 1¼ in. (3 cm) long by ¼ in. (6 mm) wide, prominently toothed, hairy. Flowers rose-lilac to rose-purple, ¾ in. (2 cm) wide, late spring to early summer.

Moderate growing; space 8–14 in. (20–35 cm) apart. Slightly acidic to slightly alkaline, well-drained, sandy loam. Drought tolerant but appreciates constantly moist soil, especially during the summer. Full sun to light shade in cool climates; light shade in warm climates.

Aurinia saxatilis
Basket-of-gold, golden alyssum

This tough, colorful, old-fashioned herb is useful as a small-scale ground cover or accent plant. In herbaceous borders with such companions as sedum, candytuft, hen and chickens, and juniper, it adds textural contrast and seasonal color. In a rock garden it may be used as a specimen, and atop a retaining wall it displays its prolific, cascading flower-topped branches. It declines and dies if exposed to prolonged heat. Zones 4–8. Europe.

A low-growing herb 6–10 in. (15–25 cm) tall, spreading 12–18 in. (30–45 cm) wide. Leaves spatula shaped to linear, evergreen, grayish green, covered with white hairs on both sides, 2–5 in. (5–13 cm) long by ½ in. (12 mm) wide. Flowers bright yellow, ¼ in. (6 mm) wide, spring.

Slow growing; space 10–14 in. (25–35 cm) apart. Nearly any acidic to neutral well-drained soil. Drought tolerant. Full sun to light shade. Prune plantings after flowering to promote branching and to stimulate new growth.

'Citrinum', many light yellow flowers.

'Compactum', most frequently cultivated, light yellow flowers, dense habit.

'Dudley Nevill Variegated', leaves with grayish white edges, flowers creamy apricot.

'Flore Pleno', double flowers, slower growing.

Gold Ball (syn. 'Goldkugel'), globelike habit.

'Golden Globe', bright yellow flowers.

'Plenum', double yellow flowers.

'Silver Queen', lemon yellow flowers, compact habit.

'Sulphureum', sulfur yellow flowers.

'Sunny Border Apricot', apricot-colored flowers.

'Tom Thumb', vigorous growing, 3–6 in. (7.5–15.0 cm) tall.

Baccharis pilularis
Coyote bush

Often recommended along the U.S. West Coast and in desert areas as much for its fire-retardant properties as for its ability to cover the ground, coyote bush is frequently planted around building entrances and perimeters and along sidewalks where it can inhibit fires that might be started by cigarette butts tossed into the bushes. It also stabilizes steep sloping banks, is highly resistant to salt spray, and may be used as an all-purpose cover on a moderate to large scale. Its tolerance to heat and drought has led some authorities to claim that it is the most dependable ground cover for desert regions. Zones 7–11. Oregon, California.

A low-growing, prostrate, woody shrub 1–2 ft. (60 cm) tall, spreading 10 ft. (3 m) wide. Leaves

Baccharis pilularis 'Pigeon Point'

dark green, evergreen, $^3/_4$ in. (2 cm) long, coated with a sticky substance, toothed along their edges. Flowers whitish yellow, insignificant, summer.

Fast growing; space 3–6 ft. (90–180 cm) apart. Dry, well-drained, sandy, acidic to neutral soil. Very drought tolerant after the first year. Full sun. Mow in early spring to keep plantings neat.

Var. *consanguinea*, compact habit.

'Pigeon Point', larger, lighter green leaves, mound-forming.

'Twin Peaks #2', smaller dark green leaves, moderate growth rate, 6–12 in. (15–30 cm) high by 6 ft. (1.8 m) wide or more.

Bergenia cordifolia
Heartleaf bergenia, pig squeak
Heartleaf bergenia is well suited for use as a general cover or facing plant for small to moderate areas, where its splendid foliage and interesting flowers are visible to passersby. The attractive leaves are often used in floral arrangements. Zones 3–9. Siberia.

A low-growing herb up to 12 in. (30 cm) tall, spreading 1–2 ft. (30–60 cm) wide. Leaves thick, leathery, shiny, evergreen, 12 in. (30 cm) long by 8 in. (20 cm) wide, very deep green, turning purplish bronze in fall. Flowers nodding, clear rose-colored, $^1/_4$–$^1/_2$ in. (6–12 mm) wide, long lasting, mid spring.

Moderate to slow growing; space 12–15 in. (30–38 cm) apart. Any moderately moist but well-drained, slightly acidic to slightly alkaline soil. Tolerates short periods of drought. Protect from strong, drying winds. Full sun to light shade in cooler climates; light to moderate shade in warmer climates.

'Alba', white flowers.

'Perfecta', large purplish bronze leaves, purplish red flowers.

Brunnera macrophylla
Heartleaf brunnera
This sturdy, long-lived, large-leaved plant is a good choice for a general cover in shady or sunny locations, where it combines nicely with early flowering bulbs, hostas, astilbes, ferns, and trees with light-colored or coarse-textured bark. Zones 3–8. Caucasus Mountains, Siberia.

Bergenia cordifolia

Brunnera macrophylla

Brunnera macrophylla 'Jack Frost'

Brunnera macrophylla 'Variegata'

Calamintha nepeta 'Montrose White'

A clump-forming, mounding herb 18–24 in. (45–60 cm) tall and wide. Leaves coarse, deciduous, oval to kidney or heart shaped with sharply pointed tips, 8 in. (20 cm) wide, deep blackish green. Flowers dainty, starlike, blue, 1/8–1/4 in. (3–6 mm) wide, above the foliage, spring.

Slow growing; space 16–24 in. (40–60 cm) apart. Constantly moist but well-drained, rich, acidic to neutral loam. Full sun to moderate shade. Divide crowded plants every two or three years.

'Jack Frost', leaves with heavy silver overlay and striking green veins.

'Langtrees', leaves with silver-gray speckles.

'Looking Glass', large leaves totally silver with just a hint of green veins.

'Silver Wings', blue-green leaves marbled with silvery overlay.

'Variegata', leaves edged with a wide band of creamy white.

Calamintha nepeta
Calamint savory
Calamint savory is a good relatively low-care ground cover for small to moderate areas. Zones 5–10. Southern Europe, Mediterranean region.

A compact, bushy herb 2 ft. (60 cm) tall, indefinitely spreading. Leaves soft green, covered with gray hair, broadly oval, 3/4 in. (20 mm) long by 3/8 in. (9 mm) wide, shallowly toothed edges, pleasantly minty smelling when crushed. Flowers mintlike, white or lilac, 5/8 in. (15 mm) long, nearly obscuring the foliage, spring to mid summer.

Moderate growing; space 12–18 in. (30–45 cm) apart. Well-drained alkaline, neutral, or partially acidic soils. Provide supplemental water in hot, dry climates. Mow once in late fall.

'Blue Cloud', lavender flowers.

'Montrose White', shorter habit, pure white flowers, very heavy flowering, mid to late summer.

Subsp. *nepeta*, more robust, with larger leaves, pinkish flowers.

'White Cloud', more upright, with dense spikes of snow white flowers.

Calluna vulgaris
Heather, Scotch heather
Heather is exceptionally interesting on hillsides when mass planted, especially when variously

colored cultivars are combined. Often it is employed in shrub borders with dwarf conifers, brooms, and heaths. In rock gardens it is one of the finest specimens available. Zones 4–7. Asia Minor, Europe.

A horizontally spreading, mounding alpine shrub 18–36 in. (45–90 cm) tall, 3–4 ft. (90–120 cm) across. Leaves evergreen, tiny, scalelike, medium green, overlapping, oblong to oval, turning bronzy. Flowers urn shaped, ⅛ in. (3 mm) wide, rose-pink or purplish pink, in upright clusters 1–10 in. (2.5–25.0 cm) long, mid to late summer.

Slow to moderate growing; space 16–22 in. (40–55 cm) apart. Moisture-retentive yet well-drained, infertile, acidic, sandy gritty or sandy loamy soils. Moderately drought tolerant. Needs good air circulation but avoid strong, drying winds and excessive humidity. Water thoroughly in hot, dry climates. Full sun. Prune immediately after flowering to keep plants dense and compact.

'Alba', white flowers.

'Aurea', purple flowers, yellow leaves turning russet in winter.

'Corbett's Red', late-opening red flowers.

'County Wicklow', double pink flowers on short spikes.

'Cuprea', 12 in. (30 cm) tall, purple flowers, golden leaves turning bronzy in fall.

'Else Frye', only 8 in. (20 cm) tall, clear double white flowers, tiny dark green leaves.

'Foxii Nana', only 4 in. (10 cm) tall, purple flowers, bright green leaves.

'Golden Aurea', white flowers, golden yellow leaves.

'Golden Aureafolia', pink flowers, golden yellow leaves.

'H. E. Beale', pale pink flowers late summer to fall, vigorous habit.

'Hammondia Aurea', white flowers, new growth bright gold.

'J. H. Hamilton', to 10 in. (25 cm) tall, double pink flowers late summer to fall, dark green leaves.

'Long White', open and upright habit, white flowers, bright green leaves.

'Mrs. Pat', only 6 in. (15 cm) tall by 10 in. (25 cm) wide, lavender flowers, bright green leaves with pink tips in spring.

Calluna vulgaris

'Nana Compacta', only 6 in. (15 cm) tall, pink flowers, bright green leaves.

'Peter Sparkes', showy, deep pink flowers, excellent for cut flowers.

'Plena Multiplex', double pink flowers.

'Robert Chapman', 10 in. (25 cm) tall, rose-purple flowers, greenish yellow leaves turning reddish in winter.

'Silver Queen', lilac-pink flowers, woolly silvery leaves.

'Sister Anne', 6 in. (15 cm) tall, many pink flowers, silvery leaves.

'Spring Cream', pink flowers in fall, bright green leaves tipped cream in spring.

'Spring Torch', 12 in. (30 cm) tall, pink flowers.

Campanula carpatica
Carpathian bellflower

Carpathian bellflower is a good ground cover for small contained, sunny areas and is superb for facing dark-leaved shrubs. The light green foliage lends a refreshing contrast and in summer the bright, crisp flowers bring yet another element of color variation. Zones 3–8. Carpathian Mountains.

A low-growing, rhizomatous herb 8–10 in. (20–25 cm) tall by 18 in. (45 cm) wide. Leaves oval to triangular, light green, 2 in. (5 cm) long by ½ in. (12 mm) wide. Flowers bluish lilac, borne slightly above the leaves, mid summer.

Moderate growing; space 8–12 in. (20–30 cm) apart. Moist but well-drained, mildly acidic to

Campanula carpatica
Blue Clips

Campanula carpatica
White Clips

CARISSA

mildly alkaline sandy to loamy soils. May require weekly watering during summer. Full sun in northern and coastal areas, light shade further south and inland. Trim back occasionally if plants sprawl outside of their bounds.

'Alba', white flowers.

'Blue Carpet', deep blue flowers, shorter and more compact than the species.

Blue Clips (syn. 'Blaue Clips'), large violet-blue flowers.

'Jingle Bells', both white and blue flowers.

'Pearl Deep Blue', round habit, earlier blooming, with larger, darker blue flowers.

'Pearl White', like 'Pearl Deep Blue' but with white flowers.

'Wedgewood Blue', 6 in. (15 cm) tall, pale blue-violet flowers.

'White Carpet', compact habit, white flowers.

White Clips (syn. 'Weisse Clips'), white flowers.

Carissa macrocarpa
Natal plum

Of greatest use in warm coastal and arid landscapes, Natal plum (formerly *Carissa grandiflora*) displays very showy fruit. Frequently it is planted atop terraces or retaining walls or in elevated planters so that its branches can cascade attractively over the sides. It is also used as edging along walkways, patio borders, and building entrances. It tolerates salty air and soil, making it valuable in coastal landscapes. Zones 7–11. South Africa.

A tough, little, shrubby plant 18–30 in. (45–75 cm) tall, spreading 3–5 ft. (90–150 cm) across. Leaves evergreen, leathery, dark green, oval, 3 in. (7.5 cm) long. Flowers funnel shaped, ½ in. (12 mm) long, waxy, white, spring. Fruit a scarlet berry, 2 in. (5 cm) in diameter.

Slow growing until rooted, then moderate growing; space 36–42 in. (90–105 cm) apart. Rich soils but tolerates mineral soils whether sandy or clay. Drought tolerant. Full sun to moderate shade. Prune out occasional upward-growing branches.

'Boxwood Beauty', compact, mound-forming to 18 in. (45 cm) tall.

'Green Carpet', 12–18 in. (30–45 cm) tall by 3–4 ft. (90–120 cm) wide.

'Horizontalis', trailing stems, densely set leaves.

'Minima', 12 in. (30 cm) tall, with leaves and flowers reduced in size.

'Prostrata', low, spreading.

'Tomlinson', shiny mahogany tinged leaves.

'Variegata', deep shiny green leaves edged in bright creamy yellow.

Carpobrotus edulis
Trailing Hottentot fig

Not to be confused with the ordinary table fig (*Ficus carica*), trailing Hottentot fig is known for its ability to cover the ground in moderate to large plantings. It is especially well suited for coastal landscaping and has few problems with shifting sand or airborne salt. On moderately sloping banks it functions well as a soil binder, but on very steep slopes the weight of the stems and leaves may cause plants to pull away from their crowns. Zones 9–11. South Africa.

A low-growing, trailing, and succulent perennial 12–18 in. (30–45 cm) tall, over 8 ft. (2.4 m) across. Leaves evergreen, 3–5 in. (7.5–13.0 cm) long by ½ in. (12 mm) wide, somewhat upward curled, gray-green with a reddish keel below. Flowers showy, solitary, to 4 in. (10 cm) across, colored light yellow, rose-pink, or purple, opening in the day, closing at night, spring.

Fast growing; space 16–24 in. (40–60 cm) apart. Any soil with excellent drainage. Withstands moderate periods of drought, but benefits from occasional deep watering. Full sun.

Ceanothus hybrids

Ceanothuses are excellent for use on large, flat or sloping surfaces. When used as specimens or in small groups for accent, they are best suited for formal landscapes. Zones 7–11.

A low-growing, wide spreading shrub. Leaves evergreen. Flowers fragrant.

Fast growing; space 3½–5 ft. (105–150 cm) apart. Light, sandy, well-drained, acidic to neutral soil. Drought tolerant for short periods; two deep waterings per month in summer are

Carissa macrocarpa

Carpobrotus edulis

Ceanothus
'Joyce Coulter'

Cephalophyllum alstonii
(photo by Richard Shiell)

Cerastium tomentosum

usually adequate. Full sun to light shade. Shear lightly each spring after blooming to keep plants looking neat and to stimulate new growth.

'**Joyce Coulter**', blue flowers, excellent for borders.

Cephalophyllum alstonii
Ice plant

Called ice plant because its foliage glistens when wet and resembles ice, this species also has magnificent flowers and is best used as a specimen in rock gardens or as a general cover on level or gently sloping terrain. It combines well with non-running succulents and herbaceous, arid-climate plants. Zones 9–11. South Africa.

A low-growing, clump-forming succulent 3–5 in. (7.5–13.0 cm) tall by 15–18 in. (38–45 cm) wide. Leaves evergreen, erect, upward curving, 2¾ in. (7 cm) long by ⅜ in. (9 mm) across, cylindrical, gray-green with dark dots. Flowers daisy-like, solitary, numerous, 3¼ in. (8 cm) wide, rich wine red, late winter to mid spring.

Moderate growing; space 6–12 in. (15–30 cm) apart. Any well-drained soil. Very drought tolerant. Full sun.

'**Red Spike**', bronzy red clawlike leaves, bright cerise-red flowers.

Cerastium tomentosum
Snow-in-summer

The flowers of this old-fashioned herb are reminiscent of newly fallen snow. The plant performs well as a general cover on a small to moderate scale, and is particularly useful on steep sunny banks, between stepping stones, and in the cracks of stone walls and ledges as a filler. Zones 3–10. Europe, Sicily.

A low-growing, creeping, matlike ground cover 6–12 in. (15–30 cm) tall by 12 in. (30 cm) wide. Leaves evergreen, oblong to lance shaped, 1 in. (2.5 cm) long by 1/4 in. (6 mm) wide, grayish green, covered with soft whitish hairs. Flowers abundant, white, 1/2–3/4 in. (12–30 mm) wide, in bundles of 3 to 15, borne above the leaves, mid to late spring.

Moderate to fast growing; 10–12 in. (25–30 cm) apart. Infertile, well-drained sandy or loamy soils. Drought tolerant. Full sun in cool climates; light shade in warm climates.

'Silver Carpet', frosty white leaves.

'Yo Yo', silvery leaves, many flowers.

Ceratostigma plumbaginoides
Dwarf plumbago, blue ceratostigma

For rich, late-season color, plumbago deserves rave reviews. Toward mid summer its gentian blue flowers begin to unfold, and by the time the first few frosts have put a damper on its cheerful floral parade, the foliage has turned a rich coppery bronze. The plant provides contrast underneath light green shrubs and small, open-canopied trees. Often it is used as an edging between paths and turf areas or as a turf substitute in tree-containing island beds of parking areas. Its assertive, spreading nature soon overruns less tenacious neighbors, but when mass planted by itself it is virtually foolproof. Zones 5–9. China.

A durable herb 6–10 in. (15–25 cm) tall, spreading indefinitely. Leaves semievergreen, usually deciduous in cool climates, oval, 1 1/2 in. (4 cm) long by 3/4 in. (2 cm) wide, emerging in late spring (frequently a full month after expected), turning burgundy, then a dull platinum green, and by season's end shades of bronze, copper, and maroon. Flowers star shaped, 1/2 in. (12 mm) wide, in dense clusters.

Ceratostigma plumbaginoides

Moderate to fast growing; space small plants 8–10 in. (20–25 cm) apart, large plants 10–16 in. (25–40 cm) apart. Rich, well-drained, acidic loam, even sandy or clay-laden soils. Water periodically during extended hot, dry weather. Full sun to moderate shade.

Chamaemelum nobile
Roman chamomile, Russian chamomile

With its apple-scented foliage and flowers, Roman chamomile is sometimes used as a turf substitute in small and moderate areas. Zones 5–9. Europe, Azores, North Africa.

Chamaemelum nobile 'Treneague'

A low-growing, horizontally spreading, dense herb 3–6 in. (7.5–15.0 cm) tall by 12 in. (30 cm) wide. Leaves bright green, evergreen, finely divided, 2 in. (5 cm) long, fernlike. Flowers tiny, in heads, daisylike with yellow centers and white petals, summer. Fruit a tiny brown seed.

Moderate to fast growing; space 10–14 in. (25–35 cm) apart. Sandy, well-drained acidic to slightly alkaline soils. Very drought tolerant. Full sun or light shade. Mow plantings during spring to rejuvenate growth and in summer, after flowering, to remove dried flower heads.

'Flore Pleno', double flowers.

'Treneague', sparsely flowering, only 2–3 in. (5.0–7.5 cm) tall.

Chelone lyonii
Lyon's turtle-head

Although used in perennial borders for many years, *Chelone* species have only recently become recognized as ground covers. As such they should be mass planted in sweeping drifts, or clumped here and there for accent. Zones 3–8.

Virginia to North Carolina, westward to Tennessee and Georgia.

An erect-stemmed, rhizomatous herb 1–3 ft. (30–90 cm) tall by 18 in. (45 cm) wide. Leaves deciduous, oval, dark green, 3–7 in. (7.5–18.0 cm) long, tip sharply pointed, base rounded, edges coarsely toothed. Flowers red or rose-purple, turtlehead shaped, 1 in. (2.5 cm) long, in numerous spikes, mid summer to early fall.

Moderate growing; space 12–18 in. (30–45 cm) apart. Moist, rich, acidic soils. Full sun to light shade. Shear plants to the ground in early spring before new growth.

'Hot Lips', rose-pink flowers, bronzy green leaves turning deep shiny green.

Chrysogonum virginianum
Golden star

Among the most endearing of North American ground covers, this florific charmer is excellent as an accent plant or facer in naturalized or native woodland gardens. It combines nicely with deciduous and evergreen shrubs, small open-

Chelone lyonii 'Hot Lips'

Chrysogonum virginianum

Cistus salviifolius

Clematis maximowicziana

Clivia miniata

canopied trees, and numerous clump-forming ferns and herbaceous perennials. Zones 5–9. Pennsylvania to Florida, west to Louisiana.

A herbaceous perennial 2–4 in. (5–10 cm) tall without flowers, twice as tall when in bloom, sprawling to 18 in. (45 cm) across. Leaves medium green, semievergreen, simple, oval to oblong, 1–3 in. (2.5–7.5 cm) wide, edges with round teeth, sparsely covered with hairs. Flowers vibrant, golden yellow, star shaped, borne above the leaves, profuse in spring, decreasing in number through summer and into fall.

Moderate growing; space 6–12 in. (15–30 cm) apart. Well-drained, rich, moderately acidic soils. Moderately drought tolerant; may require water in summer. Light to moderate shade, especially in warm climates.

'Eco Lacquered Spider', long purple strawberry-like runners and shiny green leaves.

'Springbrook', a dwarf strain of lower habit.

Cistus salviifolius
Sageleaf rock rose

Because of its fire resistance, sageleaf rock rose is well adapted to public areas, such as along pathways in parks and near building entrances, where cigarettes are likely to be tossed. It also makes a nice foundation facer and soil retainer for terraced or sloping locations. Useful in desert or seaside locations, it shows good resistance to very saline soils. Zones 7–9. Western Mediterranean region.

A low-spreading shrub 2 ft. (60 cm) tall by 6 ft. (1.8 m) wide. Leaves evergreen, elliptic to oblong, hairy, wrinkled, grayish green. Flowers 2 in. (5 cm) wide, with yellow centers and white petals (with yellow spots at their bases), profuse, late spring to mid summer.

Fast growing; space 30–42 in. (75–105 cm) apart. Coarse-textured, slightly alkaline, well-drained soils. Very drought tolerant. Full sun. Prune out the occasional dead branch.

'Avalanche', more vigorous spreading.

'Gold Star', with yellow star-shaped mark on the petals.

'May Snow', very floriferous.

'Prostratus', a name given to many lower growing seed strains.

Clematis maximowicziana
Sweet autumn clematis

Without support, this clematis forms a weed-resistant mulch. It is a natural choice for large, slightly or moderately inclined banks, where its trailing stems help control erosion by breaking the force of the rain. Because the tendrils cling to any narrow support structure, the plant should be used by itself. A lattice support or wire frame along a deck or building foundation converts this clematis into an effective facer. If placed in an elevated planter or alongside a retaining wall and allowed to cascade over, the brilliant fall floral display is brought to full attention, and the sweet fragrance easily picked up by air currents. Often sold as *Clematis paniculata*. Zones 4–9. Japan, China, Korea.

A semiwoody, vigorous, dense ground cover 8–14 in. (20–35 cm) tall, spreading over 10 ft. (3 m) wide. Leaves semievergreen, with three to five leaflets, each ½–2½ in. (2–6 cm) long by ½–1½ in. (12–40 cm) wide, oval to heart shaped, wine-red suffused with green in youth, aging to flat medium green. Flowers erect, 1 in. (2.5 cm) wide, white, highly fragrant, so profuse as to nearly obscure the leaves, late summer and early fall. Fruit is a persistent but not reliably produced, feathery, white seed.

Moderate to fast growing; space 18–30 in. (45–75 cm) apart. Well-drained, sandy to loamy, acidic to neutral soils. Fairly drought tolerant, but best with periodic watering in hot, dry weather. Tolerates wind. Full sun to light shade. Trim back shoots as they outgrow their bounds.

Clivia miniata
Clivia

This very attractive, graceful perennial functions beautifully along walkways as an edging or for accent, especially in high-traffic areas. Used in massed plantings, it makes a splendid general cover or facer for building foundations or taller shrubs. Zones 10–11. South Africa.

A lilylike herb 18–24 in. (45–60 cm) tall, spreading 30 in. (75 cm) across. Leaves evergreen, straplike, dark glossy green, 30 in. (75 cm) long by 2 in. (5 cm) wide. Flowers funnel shaped,

Convallaria majalis

Convallaria majalis
'Variegata'

Coprosma ×kirkii
'Variegata'

yellow inside, scarlet outside, 2–3 in. (5.0–7.5 cm) long, in groups of 12 to 20, borne above the leaves, early winter to early spring. Fruit a bright red berry 1 in. (2.5 cm) in diameter.

Slow growing; space 12–18 in. (30–45 cm) apart. Moderately moist but well-drained, rich, slightly acidic loam. Protect from strong, drying winds. Light to dense shade. Remove the leaves when they become tattered and cut off the floral stalks after the fruit drops.

Var. *citrina*, clear yellow flowers, yellow berries.

'Flame', deep orange-red flowers and broader, richer green, more robust foliage.

Var. *flava*, yellow flowers.

French hybrids, orange flowers.

'Grandiflora', larger flowers.

'Striata', leaves with white and green variegation.

Zimmerman hybrids, white flowers, sometimes with hints of red, yellow, or orange.

Convallaria majalis
Lily of the valley

With superbly fragrant flowers, lily of the valley performs beautifully underneath trees and combined with low shrubs, ferns, and robust hosta cultivars. It is commonly used as a general cover in small to large areas, and its soil-binding quality makes it particularly useful on shaded slopes. Zones 2–7. Europe, Asia, eastern North America.

A low-growing, horizontally spreading, lilylike, stemless herb 6–8 in. (15–20 cm) tall, spreading indefinitely. Leaves deciduous, fleshy, medium green, in groups of two or three, 4–8 in. (10–20 cm) long by 1–3 in. (2.5–7.5 cm) wide. Flowers numerous, bell shaped, 1/4 in. (6 mm) wide, waxy, white, superbly fragrant, mid to late spring. Fruit a small, round, orange-red poisonous berry, not produced reliably.

Moderate to fast growing; space 8–10 in. (20–25 cm) apart. Moist but well-drained, rich, moderately acidic loam. Survives extended periods of drought. Light to moderate shade.

'Fortunei', larger leaves and flowers.

'Prolificans', double flowers.

'Rosea', light purplish pink flowers and less vigorous growth.

'Variegata', leaf veins colored yellow, slow growing.

Coprosma ×*kirkii*
Creeping coprosma

Popular on the U.S. West Coast where it excels as a bank cover near the sea, this natural hybrid seems to enjoy being blasted by drying ocean breezes and does not mind airborne salt. It is sometimes found in arid regions, provided water for irrigation is available, and is occasionally used along fences and buildings as a facing to reduce maintenance and to obscure utility meters and foundation blocks. Zones 8–10. New Zealand. *Coprosma acerosa* × *C. repens*.

A woody shrub 3 ft. (90 cm) tall by over 5 ft. (1.5 m) across. Leaves evergreen, oblong to narrowly oblong, 1 1/2 in. (4 cm) long by 1/4 in. (6 mm) wide, medium to yellowish green with reddish edges. Flowers funnel shaped, insignificant, spring. Fruit an oblong drupe, to 1 1/4 in. (3 cm) long, translucent bluish with red speckles.

Moderate growing; space 3–4 ft. (90–120 cm) apart. Most soils. Very drought tolerant when established. Full sun to light shade. Shear lightly in spring to promote neatness and density.

'Variegata', leaves edged white.

Coreopsis verticillata
Threadleaf coreopsis

This long-blooming coreopsis is rugged, attractive, and very florific. It is best in broad sweeps along building foundations, walkways, and borders or in public or commercial landscapes surrounding the base of signs and statues, or adjoining entryways. A single clump in a smaller garden, herbaceous border, or island planting makes a superb accent. Zones 3–9. Central and eastern United States.

An upright, rhizomatous perennial 18 in. (45 cm) tall by 3 ft. (90 cm) wide. Leaves three-parted, very narrow, threadlike, medium green. Flowers numerous, daisylike, yellow, 1–1 1/2 in. (2.5–4.0 cm) wide, in groups of 6 to 10, early to late summer.

Coreopsis verticillata 'Moonbeam'

Coreopsis verticillata 'Zagreb'

Cornus canadensis

Cornus canadensis, fruit

Moderate growing; space 14–18 in. (35–45 cm) apart. Fertile, acidic loam. Drought tolerant. Full sun to light shade.

'Golden Gain', compact habit, many yellow flowers.

'Golden Showers', larger, brighter yellow flowers.

'Grandiflora', more or less identical to 'Golden Showers'.

'Moonbeam', the most popular cultivar, numerous light sulfur-yellow flowers from early summer to mid fall, hardy southward to Zone 8.

'Zagreb', 12 in. (30 cm) tall, cushion habit, golden flowers.

Cornus canadensis
Dwarf cornel

This dainty North American native is the smallest dogwood and displays the same leaf shape and flowers (but smaller) as the popular spring-blooming tree species, *Cornus florida*. It is best suited for use in the shade of trees and shrubs in moist cool climates, and is generally used as an accent plant or transition plant between a garden and surrounding woodland borders. Zones 2–7. Canada.

A ground-covering perennial 4–9 in. (10– 23 cm) tall, spreading indefinitely. Leaves deciduous, conspicuously veined, medium green, oval to elliptic, 1–3 in. (2.5–7.5 cm) long, turning yellow and red in fall. Flowers tiny, yellow and green, surrounded by white to greenish yellow oval bracts. Fruit a green berry, red when ripe, persisting from late summer to autumn.

Slow growing; space 8–12 in. (20–30 cm) apart. Moist, rich, acidic soil. Protect from strong, drying winds. Light to moderate shade in spring and fall, moderate to dense shade in summer.

Coronilla varia
Crown vetch

Crown vetch is a durable plant hated by some because of its aggressive spread and tendency to naturalize (in some parts of the United States, it has been deemed invasive). Those who love it admire its ability to bind steep slopes, its ease of maintenance, its ability to manufacture its own nitrogen (actually a task performed by bacteria living upon its roots), and its lovely pink and white flowers. It is best in areas that are dangerous to mow and in need of an inexpensive, informal, drought-tolerant covering. It combines well with tall grasses. Zones 4–9. Europe.

A perennial herb with a loose and informal habit. Leaves deciduous, fine-textured, emerald green, divided into two oblong leaflets, each ½ in. (12 mm) long. Flowers numerous, in dense, crownlike heads, early summer to early fall.

Very fast growing once established; space 10–14 in. (25–35 cm) apart. Acidic to neutral soils. Drought tolerant. Full sun. Mow in late winter to prevent the accumulation of dried stems which can become a fire hazard in drought.

'Emerald', leaves a richer green than the species, flowers primarily pinkish white.

COTONEASTER

Cotoneasters are woody shrubs of great utility. Generally they are durable, moderately aggressive, and resistant to drought and strong, drying winds. Some ground covering cotoneasters grow almost completely horizontally while others project upward with stiff woody branches. Their usefulness varies from covering banks and controlling erosion in moderate to large areas to standing alone as specimens. The two species described here make exceptional rock garden specimens due to their stiff, highly branched habit,

Coronilla varia

Cotoneaster adpressus

Cotoneaster horizontalis, in spring

Cotoneaster horizontalis, in fall

Crassula multicava (in foreground)

Cuphea hyssopifolia 'Rosea'

which can also be appreciated in elevated planters or retaining walls. Zones 5–8. China.

Well-drained, fertile, sandy or gritty, neutral or acidic loam. Full sun to light shade. Drought and wind tolerant. Prune in early spring to remove branches damaged in winter.

Cotoneaster adpressus
Creeping cotoneaster

A dense, horizontally creeping, coarse-textured shrub 4–10 in. (10–25 cm) tall by 4–6 ft. (1.2–1.8 m) wide. Leaves deciduous, broadly oval, with wavy edges, about ½ in. (12 mm) long, dull dark green, sometimes turning reddish in fall. Flowers small, pinkish, late spring and early summer. Fruit berrylike, shiny green, turning a lustrous shade of red during late summer or fall.

Slow growing; space 30–36 in. (90– cm) apart.

'Little Gem', 6 in. (15 cm) tall by 18 in. (45 cm) wide, seldom flowers.

'Praecox', early cotoneaster, vigorous growing to 3 ft. (90 cm) tall, flowers pink with a hint of purple.

Cotoneaster horizontalis
Rock spray cotoneaster

A low-growing, dense, horizontally spreading shrub 2–3 ft. (60–90 cm) tall by 6–8 ft. (1.8–2.4 m) wide. Leaves deciduous to semievergreen, roundish to broadly elliptic, with a bristly tip, coarsely textured, seldom exceeding ½ in. (12 mm) long, shiny dark green, turning reddish purple in fall. Flowers tiny, pink, inconspicuous individually but very showy collectively. Fruit glossy, bright red, round, about ¼ in. (6 mm) in diameter, early fall to mid winter.

Slow growing; space 4–5 ft. (1.2–1.5 m) apart.

'Purpusilla', exceptionally low growing.

'Robusta', heavy fruiting, more vigorous-growing, more upright habit.

'Saxatilis', leaves edged in white, then pink during autumn.

Crassula multicava

Colorful in leaf and flower, this warm-climate succulent makes a nice general cover for small to medium areas. Zones 9–10. South Africa.

A perennial herb 8–10 in. (20–25 cm) tall, spreading indefinitely. Leaves evergreen, oval, shiny green, 1–3 in. (2.5–7.5 cm) long by ¾ in. (2 cm) wide. Flowers small, light pink, late winter and spring.

Fast growing; space 18–24 in. (45–60 cm) apart. Any well-drained soil. Very drought tolerant. Full sun to light shade. Trim shoots back as the plant outgrows its bounds.

Cuphea hyssopifolia
False heather, elfin herb

False heather is attractive as a dwarf hedge, massed as a ground cover, or used alone or in small groups in a rock garden. Zones 9–11. Mexico, Guatemala.

A dainty, mound-forming shrublet 6–24 in. (15–60 cm) tall. Leaves evergreen, medium green to coppery green, linear to lance shaped, ¾ in. (2 cm) long. Flowers tiny, tubular, pink to purple to white, summer.

Slow growing; space 18–24 in. (45–60 cm) apart. Well-drained, neutral to acidic soils. Needs good air circulation. Very drought tolerant. Full sun to light shade.

'Allyson', stiffly mostly horizontal stems, vibrant green foliage, rosy purple flowers.

'Charmar Pink', dark green foliage, long-blooming purplish pink flowers.

'Compacta', compact habit, shiny bright green leaves, rose-purple flowers.

'Itsy Bitsy Lilac', bright green leaves, lilac flowers.

'Itsy Bitsy White', bright green leaves, snow white flowers.

'Rosea', purple-pink flowers.

CYMBALARIA

Popular for planting in the cracks of walls, Cymbalaria species function well as general covers for small locations, particularly if the terrain is steeply sloping, where they lend a cool green, waterfall-like softness to the landscape. Zones 5–9. Europe.

Moderate growing; space 10–16 in. (25–40 cm) apart. Well-drained but moisture-retentive, acidic to slightly alkaline soil. Moderate to dense shade. Not tolerant of extreme heat.

Cymbalaria aequitriloba

Cymbalaria muralis

Cymbalaria aequitriloba
Toadflax basket ivy
A herbaceous perennial ¼–½ in. (6–12 mm) tall, sometimes mounding higher, spreading indefinitely. Leaves medium green, composed of three to five lobes, evergreen. Flowers pale violet with a purple throat, ½ in. (12 mm) long, late spring through fall.

Cymbalaria muralis
Kenilworth ivy, coliseum ivy
A trailing herb 1–2 in. (2.5–5.0 cm) tall, spreading indefinitely. Leaves succulent, light green, rounded to heart or kidney shaped, composed of three to seven lobes, evergreen, ½–1 in. (12–25 mm) long and wide. Flowers shaped liked snapdragons, lilac-blue with a yellow throat, summer to fall.

'Alba', white flowers.

'Alba Compacta', only 12 in. (30 cm) wide, leaves apple green, flowers pure white with lemon throats.

Cytisus decumbens
Prostrate broom
Outstanding in bloom, prostrate broom makes an excellent rock garden specimen or small-scale general cover and is particularly effective when planted next to a wall or in an elevated planter over which it can trail. When combined with rel-

Cytisus decumbens
(photo by John Trager)

Dalea greggii

atively drought-tolerant shrubs such as heather, juniper, and spring heath, it creates very interesting and colorful hillside plantings. Zones 6–8. Southern Europe.

A horizontal-growing, mat-forming, semi-woody perennial 8 in. (20 cm) tall (although often it stays much lower), spreading over 3 ft. (90 cm) across. Leaves tiny, deciduous, dull medium green, oblong to oval, ¼–¾ in. (6–20 mm) long by less than ⅛ in. (3 mm) wide. Flowers yellow, pealike, ½–⅝ in. (12–15 mm) long, profuse in late spring, sporadic thereafter until fall.

Moderate growing; space 16–24 in. (40–60 cm) apart. Well-drained sandy or gravelly loam. Very drought tolerant. Full sun. Tolerates wind.

Dalea greggii
Trailing indigo bush

In the United States, this species is best in southwestern deserts as a general cover and soil retainer for moderate to large scale on level or sloping ground. Zones 9–10. Mexico (Chihuahua desert).

A low, sprawling, woody shrub 12 in. (30 cm) tall, occasionally to 2 ft. (60 cm), spreading 4–8 ft. (1.2–2.4 m) across. Leaves compound, evergreen, ½ in. (12 mm) long by half as wide, divided into nine narrowly oval leaflets, gray-green covered with white hairs. Flowers small, purple, in dense round heads, spring to summer.

Moderate to fast growing; space 18–24 in. (45–60 cm) apart. Any well-drained soil. Drought

Dampiera diversifolia (photo by Pamela Harper)

tolerant when established. Full sun; tolerates light shade. Trim back the leading stems as they outgrow their bounds.

Dampiera diversifolia
Dampiera

Dampiera grows well in the cracks of a rock ledge and looks beautiful when allowed to spill over the edge, especially when in bloom. It can be mass planted and on slopes functions well as a soil binder. Dampiera is said to combine well with bulbs and with open-canopied Australian native trees and shrubs. Zones 9–10. Southwestern Australia.

A low-growing, trailing, subshrubby, semi-woody perennial 4 in. (10 cm) tall by 3–5 ft. (90–150 cm) wide. Leaves evergreen, medium green, densely set, simple, 1–2 in. (2.5–5.0 cm) long, simple, crowded, narrowly lance shaped at the base of the plant, more rounded further up the stem, edged with small teeth. Flowers ⅝ in. (15 mm) across, yellow center surrounded by five deep purplish blue (rarely pale blue) petals, fragrant in hot weather, profuse, spring and summer.

Slow growing initially, moderate growing once established; space 18–30 in. (45–75 cm) apart. Slightly moist but well-drained gravelly soils to clay loam. Light shade. Protect from strong, drying winds. Shear lightly after flowering to keep plants neat and compact.

DELOSPERMA
Hardy ice plant

Remarkable for their colorful, daisylike flowers and glistening foliage, hardy ice plants are attractive either as single, sprawling specimens for accent, or in larger masses. They can be combined with drought-tolerant dwarf evergreens and, when used for facing, they draw attention to garden statuary, public fountains and pools, and building entrances. A few flats of variously colored, upright-growing, clump-forming stonecrops interspersed among ice plants will create a beautiful montage of color.

Moderate growing; space 12–16 in. (30–40 cm) apart. Any well-drained soil. Very drought tolerant. Full sun.

Delosperma congestum 'Gold Nugget'

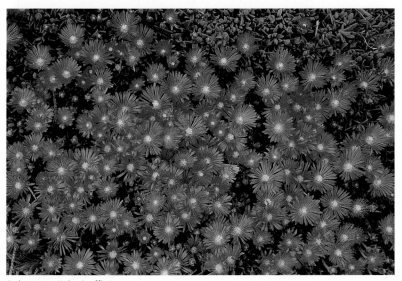

Delosperma 'John Proffitt'

Delosperma congestum 'Gold Nugget'

A slow-creeping, compact selection. Leaves evergreen, succulent, ³⁄₄ in. (2 cm) long, light apple green. Flowers daisylike, sunny yellow, nearly obscuring the foliage during spring.

Delosperma 'John Proffitt'

A mat-forming ice plant 1–2 in. (2.5–5.0 cm) tall, spreading over 2 ft. (60 cm) across. Leaves elongate, evergreen, rubbery, water filled, dark green, 1 in. (2.5 cm) long. Flowers daisylike, bright fuchsia-red, above the foliage and nearly obscuring it, spring.

Delosperma nubigena

Deutzia gracilis 'Nikko'

Dianthus Firewitch

Delosperma nubigena
Cloud-loving hardy ice plant

A mossy, cheerfully colored, carpeting ice plant less than 2 in. (5 cm) tall by up to 3 ft. (90 cm) wide. Leaves evergreen, bright, light, shiny green, 1¼ in. (3 cm) long by 3/16 in. (5 mm) wide, thick, fleshy, sometimes turning reddish in fall. Flowers numerous, daisylike, almost chartreuse-yellow, exceptionally bright, ¾ in. (2 cm) wide, spring. Zones 5–10. Drakensberg Mountains of South Africa.

Fast growing; space 10–14 in. (25–35 cm) apart.

'Basutoland', smaller flowers.

Deutzia gracilis 'Nikko'
Nikko deutzia

Mass planted on a moderate to large scale, Nikko deutzia conceals partially exposed foundations, and its habit of rooting allows it to excel as a soil binder on moderately inclined slopes. It makes an exceptional specimen alongside stairs, in planters, or atop retaining walls. Nikko deutzia combines well with other dwarf shrubs in border plantings and looks especially attractive in front of taller shrubs with deep green leaves. Zones 5–8. Japan.

A tenacious-spreading, compact, low-growing shrub 18–30 in. (45–75 cm) tall by 5 ft. (1.5 m) across. Leaves deciduous, narrow, oblong to lance shaped, medium green, 1¾–2¼ in. (45–56 mm) long by 3/8–5/8 in. (9–15 mm) wide, edges toothed, fall color often purplish. Flowers numerous, showy, tiny, white, in clusters 1 in. (2.5 cm) across, late spring.

Moderate to fast growing; space 30–42 in. (75–105 cm) apart. Well-drained, sandy to clay loam, acidic soils. Moderately drought tolerant; water during extended periods of hot, dry weather. Full sun to light shade in cool climates; full sun with afternoon shade in warm climates. Shear lightly after flowering to promote compact growth.

Dianthus hybrids
Carnations

Dianthus is a large genus of approximately 300 mat-forming herbs that offer some of the most beautifully flowered ground covers in cultivation. These are true carnations, the kind you buy from a florist, yet compact growing and cold hardy. Adorable for their petite highly fragrant flowers and tufted grasslike habit, carnations also tend to be disease prone and demanding in respect to maintenance. For this reason they are usually used on a small scale. Like all long-appreciated florific plants, carnations have been extensively hybridized and it is uncertain whether these are hybrid cultivars or cultivars of cottage pink. Since most of the species originated in Europe, I follow European authors in listing these as hybrid cultivars. Zones 3–9.

Leaves evergreen, narrow, grasslike. Flowers fragrant, rose or pink, ¾ in. (2 cm) wide, spring, may repeat bloom in late summer.

Slow to moderate growing; space 8–14 in. (20–35 cm) apart. Well-drained, neutral to alkaline soil. Needs water during hot summer weather. Full sun to light shade. Divide overcrowded plants every two or three years. Prune flowers after blooming to neaten appearance.

'**Bath's Pink**', soft pink, fringed flowers.

'**Dottie**', 4–5 in. (10–13 cm) tall, maroon and white flowers.

'**Double Cheddar**', double pink flowers.

Firewitch (syn. 'Feuerhexe'), dense habit, blue foliage, 8 in. (20 cm) tall, covered with raspberry red flowers.

'**Petite**', to 4 in. (10 cm) tall, pink flowers.

'**Pink Feather**', feathery pink flowers.

'**Spotty**', rose-red flowers edged and spotted with silvery white.

Dicentra hybrids
Bleeding heart

Among the most popular and useful ground covers for shade gardens, bleeding heart can be used as a specimen or in small groups for accent, particularly in highly visible locations where its grace and charm can best be appreciated. Often it is combined with ferns, trillium, columbine, spring beauty, hepatica, and blood root. Zones 3–9.

Leaves typically compound or deeply dissected and fernlike. Flowers with flattened heart-shaped corollas, in racemose clusters, usually nodding upon succulent stalks, spring to fall.

Dicentra 'Ivory Hearts'

Dicentra 'King of Hearts'

Disporum sessile 'Variegatum'

Drosanthemum floribundum

Slow growing; space 12–16 in. (30–40 cm) apart. Moist but well-drained, rich, moderately acidic soils. Light to moderate shade.

'Ivory Hearts', like 'King of Hearts' but with white flowers.

'King of Hearts', to 12 in. (30 cm) tall, powdery blue foliage topped with rosy pink flowers.

Disporum sessile
Japanese fairy bells

Japanese fairy bells is used for accent or general cover, and in the case of the variegated selection, which is more popular than the species, for contrast against shrubs with dark green leaves. Walkway and border edging are also good uses, provided some type of barrier contains the plant's spread. Zone 5. China, Japan.

A rhizomatous, gracefully arching herb 14–24 in. (35–60 cm) tall and spreading indefinitely. Leaves deciduous, simple, oblong to lance shaped, 4 in. (10 cm) long by 1 in. (2.5 cm) wide. Flowers nodding, bell shaped, creamy white, spring.

Slow to moderate growing; space 12–16 in. (30–40 cm) apart. Well-drained, rich, moderately acidic loam. Drought tolerant. Cool temperatures. Light to moderate shade.

'Variegatum', creamy white edges and longitudinal stripes.

Drosanthemum floribundum
Rosy ice plant

Rosy ice plant is useful around shrubs and building foundations, and helps to control erosion on rocky slopes. The floral show it puts on during spring and summer is absolutely breathtaking. The water-filled leaves reflect light. Zones 9–10. South Africa.

A matlike, trailing succulent 6 in. (15 cm) tall, spreading indefinitely. Leaves evergreen, ½ in. (12 mm) long by ⅛ in. (3 mm) wide, covered with pimplelike protrusions, grayish. Flowers bright pink, ¾ in. (2 cm) across, spring and summer.

Fast growing; space 12–18 in. (30–45 cm) apart. Any well-drained soil. Very drought tolerant.

Duchesnea indica

Duchesnea indica, flowers and fruits (courtesy of Walters Gardens.

Duchesnea indica
Mock strawberry, Indian strawberry

Mock strawberry is valuable as a small-scale turf substitute, and it combines well with various small trees and shrubs. It is a good soil stabilizer on steeply sloping banks. Zones 4–8. Southern Asia.

A low-growing, mat-forming herb 2 in. (5 cm) tall, spreading indefinitely. Leaves evergreen, composed of three leaflets, each one oval, 1 in. (2.5 cm) long by ½ in. (12 mm) wide, coarsely toothed around the edges, somewhat hairy, medium green with a reddish base. Flowers ½–1 in. (12–25 mm) long, yellow, and borne intermittently throughout the growing season. Fruit strawberry shaped, red, ½ in. (12 mm) in diameter, bland to bitter tasting but attractive to birds.

Fast growing; space 14–18 in. (35–45 cm) apart. Any well-drained soil. Very drought tolerant. Light shade but tolerates full sun if soil is kept moist. Mow plantings in early spring to stimulate new growth and to neaten appearance.

'Variegata', leaves edged white.

Echeveria elegans
Mexican gem, Mexican snowball

Typically used in rock gardens as an accent or specimen plant, Mexican gem has extraordinarily colorful leaves. In some cases it performs remarkably well as a general cover in small to moderate areas. Zones 9–11. Mexico.

A rosette-forming succulent 3 in. (7.5 cm) tall. Leaves 1½– 2½ in. (4–6 cm) long by 1 in. (2.5 cm) wide. bluish green with translucent edges. Flowers rose-red with yellow tips, late winter to early summer.

Moderate growing; space 6–10 in. (15–25 cm) apart. Well-drained sandy or gritty soils. Drought tolerant. Full sun to light shade.

EPIMEDIUM

Epimediums are marvelous edging plants for walkways, garden paths, alongside steps, and around the periphery of herbaceous border plantings. Single clumps or small groupings make excellent specimen or accent plants along woodland borders, and mass plantings are superb for facing garden ornaments, trees, and building foundations.

Echeveria elegans

Epimedium alpinum 'Rubrum'

Slow to moderate growing; space 10–12 in. (25–30 cm) apart. Well-drained, rich, slightly acidic loam. Drought tolerant but better with periodic watering in mid summer. Light to moderate shade.

Epimedium alpinum
Alpine epimedium

A dense, erect-growing perennial 10–15 in. (25–38 cm) tall. Leaves deciduous to semievergreen, leathery, heart shaped, tapering to a fine point, 5 in. (13 cm) long, pinkish in youth, then medium green before becoming bronzy in fall. Flowers nodding, ½ in. (12 mm) wide, with red sepals and yellow petals, often partially obscured by foliage, mid spring. Zones 3–8. Southern and central Europe.

'Rubrum', sepals brighter red and petals brighter yellow than the species.

Epimedium ×youngianum

The result of a cross between Epimedium diphyllum and E. grandiflorum, this spring-flowering hybrid has given rise to some very fine cultivars that reach 8–15 in. (20–38 cm) tall.

'Niveum', dainty light to medium green foliage, many snow white flowers.

'Roseum', leaves red streaked in spring, green in summer, and burgundy red in fall; many rosy red pendulous flowers.

'Sulphureum', medium green foliage, sulfur yellow flowers.

Erica carnea
Spring heath

A close cousin to heather, spring heath is excellent on a small to large scale for sloping, sandy or gravelly terrain. It can be combined with slow-

Epimedium ×youngianum
'Niveum'

Epimedium ×youngianum
'Sulphureum'

growing, acid-loving shrublets and ground covers to create brilliantly colorful, multitextured lawn substitutes or foundation facers. Spring heath is exceptional in the rock garden, atop a rock retaining wall, or combined with herbaceous perennials in a border. It tolerates salt and thus is useful in coastal gardens. Zones 5–7 (reliable snow cover and shelter from winter wind needed in the extreme northern part of this range). Central and southern Europe.

A small, woody, dense, horizontally spreading subshrub 12 in. (30 cm) tall, spreading 18–24 in. (45–60 cm) across. Leaves tiny, needlelike, evergreen, ¼ in. (6 mm) long, shiny, dark green. Flowers ¼ in. (6 mm) long, urn shaped, red to whitish, late winter to early spring.

Slow growing; space 14–20 in. (35–50 cm) apart. Well-drained, acidic, sandy or loamy soils.

Needs occasional deep watering in drought. Best with high humidity and cool to moderate temperatures. Full sun.

'**Alan Coates**', compact habit, pale rose-colored flowers maturing to purple.

'**Aurea**', deep pink flowers, light lime green leaves becoming golden yellow in winter.

'**December Red**', vigorous habit, 6–9 in. (15–23 cm) tall, red flowers.

'**Foxhollow Fairy**', white and pink flowers maturing to deep pink, light green foliage.

'**King George**', deep rose-pink flowers.

'**Myretoun Ruby**', ruby red flowers.

'**Pink Spangles**', unique lilac and deep pink bicolored flowers.

'**Springwood Pink**', white flowers maturing to clear pink.

'**Springwood White**', white flowers.

Erica carnea
'Springwood Pink'

Erica carnea
'Springwood White'

'Vivelli', almost blood-red flowers, dark green foliage becoming bronzy in winter.

Erigeron karvinskianus
Bonytip fleabane

The homely common name fails to portray the beauty of the magnificent, multicolored flowers. Of great utility in hot, arid climates, bonytip fleabane tolerates high salinity and drought, and is very useful as a moderate-scale general cover around and underneath large shrubs and small trees. Because of its rambling nature, it should be used in areas that naturally check its spread and never with smaller shrubs and herbs that it can overrun. Zones 9–11. Mexico to Venezuela.

A low-growing, trailing herb 10–20 in. (25–50 cm) tall. Leaves evergreen, elliptic to oval, often lobed, often edged with teeth, medium green, 1 1/4 in. (3 cm) long by 1/2 in. (12 mm) wide. Flowers sunflower-like, 3/4 in. (2 cm) wide, center yellow, petals white turning pink then finally reddish purple, throughout the growing season.

Fast growing; space 14–20 in. (35–50 cm) apart. Infertile, well-drained, acidic or alkaline sandy loam. Drought tolerant, although it appreciates an occasional deep watering in summer. Full sun. Mow in late fall to keep plantings neat.

'Profusion', tiny pink and white flowers.

'Spindrift', 8–10 in. (20–25 cm) tall with less tendency to reseed.

'Stallone', only 12 in. (30 cm) tall by 24 in. (60 cm) wide.

Euonymus fortunei
Wintercreeper

As an evergreen climber, wintercreeper may reach 20 ft. (6 m), but if not given support, it becomes a very thick, very useful ground cover. Even so, the species is seldom seen because its cultivars and varieties are better still. The dwarf, small-leaved varieties are best for general use on a small scale where a dense carpet is needed. In planters, alongside steps, and trailing over walls, the colorful variegated selections are quite useful. Larger forms, with their greater vigor, are excellent on a moderate to large scale, especially on

hillsides where their extensive root systems help to check erosion. Zones 4–9. China.

Adult foliage thicker, more leathery, and more rounded than the juvenile foliage, but seldom observed unless the stems have ascended high above the ground, triggering the maturation process. Juvenile leaves evergreen, paired, elliptic to oval, to 2 in. (5 cm) long, edged with broad, shallow or rounded teeth, dark green with prominent silvery white veins. Flowers small, greenish, on mature branches, insignificant. Fruit a pinkish capsule, very ornamental, fall through winter.

Moderately to relatively fast growing; space 10–36 in. (25–90 cm) apart, 12–24 in. (30–60 cm) apart if a dwarf form. Acidic to slightly alkaline loam. Benefits from an occasional deep watering in summer. Full sun to relatively dense shade. Trim back the leading stems as they outgrow their designated bounds.

'Acutus', narrow, dark green leaves, vigorous habit.

'Canadian Variegated', small, medium green leaves with white edges.

'Coloratus', purple wintercreeper, the most popular selection in North America, dark green foliage with purplish fall and winter color, rapid growth, rooting stems that are exceptional for binding soil.

'Emerald Gaiety', sprawling habit to 18 in. (45 cm), green and cream leaves turn pinkish red in fall and winter.

'Emerald 'n' Gold', leaves relatively small, dark, glossy green with yellow edges, developing reddish tints in fall.

'Harlequin', a somewhat weak grower with foliage irregularly splotched and flecked white and green.

'Kewensis', leaves only 1/4–1/2 in. (6–12 mm) long, plant height 2–3 in. (5.0–7.5 cm).

'Longwood', 4 in. (10 cm) tall, small leaves.

'Moon Shadow', stems yellow, leaves with yellow centers and wavy green margins.

Var. radicans 'Argenteo-Variegata', dark green leaves edged in silvery white.

'Sparkle 'n' Gold', to 3 ft. (90 cm) tall by 6 ft. (1.8 m) wide, dark green leaves with broad bright yellow edges.

*Erigeron
karvinskianus*

Euonymus fortunei
'Coloratus'

Euonymus fortunei
'Emerald 'n' Gold'

'Sun Spot', dark green leaves with a vibrant yellow spot in the center.

'Tricolor', white, cream, and green leaves that take on hints of pink and red during fall.

EUPHORBIA

Euphorbias bear unusual poinsettia-like flowers in clusters at the tips of the branches. They perform beautifully as edging along a formal walk or winding garden path, as a specimen in rock gardens or borders, planted atop retaining walls, or massed in moderate expanses as a facing or general cover. Zones 4–8. Eastern Europe.

Moderate growing; space 14–20 in. (35–50 cm) apart. Loose, sandy or gravelly, well-drained neutral to alkaline soils. Very drought tolerant. Full sun to moderate shade; light to moderate shade (or at least afternoon shade) in hot summer locations. Shear lightly after flowering to keep plantings compact and neat.

Euphorbia amygdaloides

Leaves deep glossy green. Floral bracts light green, loose habit, spring, 20 in. (50 cm) tall.

'Purpurea', deep purple-red stems, blue-green foliage turning purplish in spring and fall.

'Red Wing', red buds, yellow-green flowers.

Var. *robbiae*, rhizomatous spreader.

'Rubra', reddish green leaves turning rich purple in fall.

Euphorbia amygdaloides
'Purpurea'

Euphorbia amygdaloides
var. *robbiae*

Euphorbia ×martinii

A natural hybrid 18 in. (45 cm) tall. Leaves narrowly teardrop shaped, reddish tinged, 1½–2 in. 4–5 cm) long, on tight branches. Floral bracts light green, above the foliage, in loose upright inflorescences, early summer. Zones 7–10. *Euphorbia amygdaloides* × *E. characias*.

'Mini Martini', only 10 in. (25 cm) tall.

Fallopia japonica
Japanese fleeceflower

Some consider this species an overbearing thug, which it is if incorrectly paired. It should be employed as a low hedge or walkway border where it can be contained or as a large-scale blanket (par-

ticularly on slopes) where it can spread and bind soil, the two real joys of its long life. In cool climates, as a border around parking lots or alongside building entrances or walks, Japanese fleeceflower is an excellent choice as it withstands drought, heat, reflected summer sun, and radiant heat from the pavement. In winter it dies back, thus saving itself from the snow plow damage customarily associated with such plantings. Zones 3–10. Japan.

A sprawling, rhizomatous, deciduous herb 18–36 in. (45–90 cm) tall, spreading indefinitely. Leaves simple, entire, variously shaped, usually 3–4 in. (7.5–10.0 cm) long, oval, leathery, medium green, but reddish in youth, crimson in fall. Flowers numerous, white, in dense clusters.

Euphorbia ×*martinii*

Fallopia japonica
'Compacta'

Fallopia japonica
'Variegata'

Felicia amelloides
(photo by Pamela Harper)

Ficus pumila
'Variegata'

Relatively fast growing; space 16–24 in. (40–60 cm) apart. Any well-drained soil. Very drought tolerant.

'**Compacta**', compact habit, red buds, pink-and-white flowers in late summer and early fall, fruit with pink-and-red winglike appendages—about six weeks of sensational color and a great way to finish out the growing season.

'**Variegata**', taller than the species, tends to stay in a sprawling clump, exceptional for brightening up shady hillsides and borders.

Felicia amelloides
Blue marguerite, blue daisy

A single plant makes a showy specimen in a rock garden or perennial border, and mass plantings are striking. As an edging, atop retaining walls, and in raised planters (and allowed to trail over), blue marguerite is excellent. Zones 9–10. South Africa.

A sprawling, semiwoody subshrub 18–36 in. (45–90 cm) tall, spreading over 5 ft. (1.5 m) across. Leaves evergreen, oblong to oval or elliptic, 1–1¼ in. (25–30 mm) long by ½ in. (12 mm) wide. Flowers daisylike, sky blue with yellow centers, 1⅜ in. (35 mm) wide, early summer through fall.

Moderate to fast growing; space 36–42 in. (90–105 cm) apart. Moderately rich, well-drained soil. Drought tolerant. Full sun to light shade. A hard shearing following bloom enhances its appearance and may induce further flowering.

'**Astrid Thomas**', medium blue flowers.
'**Golden Sapphires**', only 18 in. (45 cm) tall.
'**Jolly**', medium blue flowers, dwarf habit.
'**Midnight**', deep blue flowers.
'**Read's Blue**', large blue flowers with golden centers.
'**Read's White**', white flowers with golden centers.
'**Rhapsody in Blue**', dark blue flowers.
'**Santa Anita**', large blue flowers.
'**Santa Anita Variegata**', large blue flowers, stippled leaves.

Ficus pumila
Creeping fig, climbing fig

Creeping fig, one of my favorites for a small-scale cover in warm climates, is a true fig. It is often planted in contained areas and elevated planters. It forms splendid green carpets and makes a fine setting for shrubby and treelike figs and palms, and tall clump-forming tropical herbs. Zones 8–10. China, Japan, Australia, Vietnam.

A small, neatly leaved woody vine ½–1½ in. (12–40 mm) tall when unsupported, spreading indefinitely. Juvenile leaves heart shaped to oval, evergreen, 1 in. (2.5 cm) long, glossy green. Adult leaves oblong or elliptical, 2–4 in. (5–10 cm) long, thicker, leathery, on very stout branches. Flowers tiny. Fruit pear shaped, inedible, 2 in. (5 cm) long, orange, then red-purple.

Tentative growing initially, fast growing once well rooted; space 14–36 in. (35–90 cm) apart. Moist, rich loam. Tolerates short periods of drought. Full sun to light shade, but avoid the extreme heat and light of a southern or western exposure. Cut back branches as they outgrow their bounds.

'**Minima**', smaller leaves.
'**Snowflake**', leaves with broad, snow white edges.
'**Variegata**', leaves with attractive white edges.

FRAGARIA
Strawberry

This genus, in addition to producing delicious fruits, also gives us some splendid ground covers for binding soil on gradually sloping banks, as turf substitutes on a small to moderate scale, in naturalized, lightly shaded woodland settings, and as facings to large shrubs and trees. Zones 4–9. Europe, North and South America.

Moderate to fast growing; space 8–14 in. (20–35 cm) apart. Any well-drained soil. Relatively drought tolerant; best in slightly moist soil. Full sun to light shade. Mow plantings during late winter to promote density and to renew vigor.

Fragaria 'Lipstick'

Fragaria vesca

Fragaria hybrids

Interesting hybrids have been formed by crossing unknown species of *Fragaria* and *Potentilla*. The result is a strawberry-like plant with beautiful, large, deep pink flowers. Zone 5.

'Lipstick', deep pink flowers.

'Pink Panda', strawberry potentilla, produces an occasional edible fruit.

Shades of Pink, a mixed group of seedlings with light to dark pink flowers.

Fragaria vesca
European strawberry, woodland strawberry

A perennial herb to 8 in. (20 cm) tall, spreading indefinitely. Leaves evergreen, three-parted, to 2½ in. (5 cm) long. Flowers ⅜–¾ in. (9–20 mm) wide, white, spring. Fruit red, edible but not as flavorful as garden strawberries. Zones 5–10. European Alps.

Var. *albicarpa* (syn. 'Fructo-alba'), white fruit.

'Alexandria', dwarf, nonrunning habit.

'Multiplex', small double white flowers.

Var. *semperflorens*, nearly without runners, blooming spring through late summer.

'Variegata', leaves with striking white and green variegation.

Francoa ramosa
Maiden's wreath, bridal wreath

Although not widely cultivated, maiden's wreath is useful as a specimen or background plant in the perennial border. It prefers dry winter cli-

Francoa ramosa

Galium odoratum

mates and is best in naturalistic settings. It also is an attractive cut flower. Zones 8–10. Chile.

A basal-leaved, clump-forming, rhizomatous herb 1–2 ft. (30–60 cm) tall, spreading 2–3 ft. (60–90 cm) across. Leaves mostly evergreen, leathery, lyre shaped, 6–12 in. (15–30 cm) long by 2–3 in. (5.0–7.5 cm) wide, edged with irregular, wavy lobes, surface smooth, medium green to gray-green above, with hairy veins on the underside. Flowers white, ¾ in. (2 cm) wide, in terminal racemes 6–12 in. (15–30 cm) long, elevated well above the foliage, mid summer.

Moderate growing; space 24–30 in. (60–75 cm) apart. Most well-drained soils. Good drought tolerance. Light to moderate shade. Remove the flower stalks after the blossoms fade to neaten the plant's appearance.

Galium odoratum
Sweet woodruff, bedstraw

Sweet woodruff provides soft texture and uniform growth underneath shallowly rooted trees and shrubs, and can be used as a general cover for small to large areas. It thrives in very dense shade where few other plants can survive and combines well with spring-flowering bulbs, hostas, and ferns. Occasionally, it is used as an edging for a perennial border or garden path. Zones 4–8. Europe, Asia.

A low, horizontally spreading, upright herb 6–10 in. (15–25 cm) tall, spreading indefinitely. Leaves medium green, semievergreen or deciduous (depending on the climate), oval to narrowly oval, 1½ in. (4 cm) long, edges minutely toothed. Flowers tiny, white, mildly fragrant, in

A shrub 1–2 ft. (30–60 cm) tall, spreading 2–4 ft. (60–120 cm) wide. Leaves dark glossy green, evergreen, oval, 1–2 in. (2.5–5.0 cm) long by ½–1 in. (12–25 mm) wide, often streaked with white, thick, leathery. Flowers waxy, white, exceptionally fragrant, 1 in. (2.5 cm) across, mid summer to early fall. Fruit an oval, orange, fleshy berry.

Slow growing; space 18–30 in. (45–75 cm) apart. Rich, well-drained, acidic loam. Very drought tolerant. Full sun to moderate shade. Mulch yearly above the roots to help keep them cool and to conserve water.

Gardenia jasminoides 'Radicans' (courtesy of Master Tag Corporation)

Gaultheria procumbens

clusters 1 in. (2.5 cm) in diameter, mid to late spring.

Moderate growing; space 8–12 in. (20–30 cm) apart. Moist but well-drained, rich, acidic loam. Protect from strong winds. Moderate to dense shade.

Gardenia jasminoides 'Radicans'
Creeping Cape-jasmine

Best in small to medium plantings as a general cover, creeping Cape jasmine is especially nice as a foundation facer or filler inside elevated planters or terrace embankments. Zones 8–10. China.

GAULTHERIA
Wintergreen

Wintergreen is one of the most durable, aesthetically pleasing, and widely distributed North American natives; yet its resistance to propagation and fussiness for soil type limit its widespread landscape use. Many wintergreens possess aromatic foliage and edible fruit. They combine wonderfully with other taller-growing, acid-loving plants, are most at home in woodland gardens, and make superb edging to woodland paths and borders.

Relatively organic, acidic soil of constant moisture, including sandy soils. Light to moderate shade.

Gaultheria procumbens
Common wintergreen, winterberry

A low-growing, creeping, semiherbaceous, subshrub 3–5 in. (9–13 cm) tall, spreading indefinitely. Leaves light green, evergreen, becoming tough, leathery, and shiny dark green within a few months after emerging, elliptic to narrowly oval at maturity, 2 in. (5 cm) long by 1¼ in. (3 cm) across, aromatic, turning purple in fall. Flowers resemble little nodding, pinkish white urns, mid spring. Fruit is a fleshy, pleasant-tasting, round, scarlet berry. Zones 3–7. Eastern North America.

Slow growing; space 10–14 in. (25–35 cm) apart. Difficult to propagate.

Gaultheria shallon
Salal, shallon

Florists use the branches and leaves of salal in flower arrangements.

A rhizomatous shrub 3–4 ft. (90–120 cm) tall, spreading over 3 ft. (90 cm) across. Leaves deep green, roughened, oval to nearly round, evergreen, 4 in. (10 cm) wide, edges rough. Flowers white or pinkish, bell shaped, late spring to early summer. Fruit purple, ripening to black by late summer. Zone 7 or 8. Western North America.

Slow growing; space 14–24 in. (34–60 cm) apart.

Gaultheria shallon

Gazania rigens
Trailing gazania

Marvelously utilitarian, trailing gazania is excellent for edging walkways and driveways and as a turf substitute around paved areas. It is useful on a moderate to large scale around building foundations, in front of stone walls and fences as a facing plant, and on moderately sloping embankments for soil retention. Zones 8–10. South Africa.

A rugged herb 6–8 in. (15–20 cm) tall, spreading indefinitely. Leaves evergreen, elongated, 4–5 in. (10–13 cm) long by ½ in. (12 mm) wide, gray-green above, covered with white hairs below, in attractive rosettelike arrangements. Flowers daisylike, 3 in. (7.5 cm) wide, orange with a dark brown, white-dotted splotch in the center, spring through summer.

Moderate to fast growing; space 10–14 in. (25–35 cm) apart. Any well-drained soil. Drought tolerant, but often requires watering during extended dry periods. Full sun. Mow after flowering to neaten appearance and to stimulate new growth.

Gazania rigens cultivars

Gazania hybrids

The horticultural selections are so many and so terribly mixed up that they are often categorized by hybrid group. Those described here represent a portion of what is offered. Most are probably hybrids (sometimes listed as cultivars of *Gazania splendens*, probably the same thing as *G. rigens*).

'Aztec Queen', a group of multicolored selections.

Gazania 'Mitzuwa Yellow'

Gelsemium sempervirens (photo by Stephen Still)

'Colorama', flowers to 4 in. (10 cm) wide in mixed colors.

'Copper King', orange flowers and markings in various colors.

'Fiesta Red', dark reddish orange flowers.

'Fire Emerald', flowers in various colors but characteristically with emerald green petal bases.

'Gold Rush', orange-yellow flowers and brown basal spots.

'Mini Star White', snow white flowers with brown petal bases and yellow centers.

'Mitzuwa Yellow', yellow flowers.

'Moon Glow', double yellow flowers.

'Sunburst', orange flowers with black centers, leaves gray.

'Sunglow', yellow flowers.

Gelsemium sempervirens
Carolina jessamine

The state flower of South Carolina is best as a general cover in large areas where it will not interfere with shrubs and trees, such as sloping highway embankments and medians. On a smaller scale, it can be planted next to a retaining wall over which the stems can cascade gracefully and breezes can pick up the marvelous fragrance of the flowers. Zones 7–9. Eastern North America from Virginia south.

A shrubby, twining vine 3 ft. (90 cm) tall when unsupported, spreading 20–30 ft. (6–9 m) across. Leaves semievergreen to evergreen, dark shiny green, relatively long and narrow, to 4 in. (10 cm) long by 1¼ in. (3 cm) wide, purplish in winter. Flowers bright yellow, trumpet shaped, fragrant, 1½ in. (4 cm), late winter to early spring, sometimes sporadically again in fall.

Moderate growing; space 3–4 ft. (90–120 cm) apart. Rich, fertile, well-drained, acidic loam. Tolerates short periods of drought, yet appreciates an occasional deep watering during the summer. Full sun. The leaves, bark, stems, roots, and flowers are poisonous when ingested.

'Pride of Augusta' (syn. 'Plena'), double flowering, with the normal spring bloom period extending into summer.

Genista pilosa

Genista pilosa
Silky-leaf woadwaxen

Very good for covering up the soil and as a turf substitute on a small to moderate scale, silky-leaf woadwaxen is employed more often as an interesting rock garden or perennial border specimen, where it combines well with heaths, heathers, carnations, and bell flowers. It is excellent on slopes and terraces, and in planters. Zones 6–8. Europe.

A shrub 12 in. (30 cm) tall, rooting along its branches as it spreads. Leaves very small, simple, deciduous, medium green to silvery green. Flowers pealike, bright yellow, in terminal clusters, early summer. Fruit reminiscent of a miniature pea pod.

Slow to moderate growing; space 6–27 in. (15–68 cm) apart. Alkaline to partially acidic, infertile, well-drained, sandy or rocky soils. Very drought tolerant, but prefers an occasional deep watering in summer. Full sun to light shade. Needs good air circulation. Prune lightly after flowering for a neat, compact habit.

'Gold Flash', golden yellow flowers, very durable, Zones 3–8.

Var. *procumbens*, 2 in. (5 cm) tall by 3 ft. (90 cm) wide.

'Vancouver Gold', a popular cultivar that does not set seed, 4–6 in. (10–15 cm) tall by 3–4 ft. (90–120 cm) wide; dark green leaves, numerous golden yellow flowers from late spring to early summer.

GERANIUM
Cranesbill

The "true" geraniums—not the so-called geraniums you buy in hanging baskets each spring or grow in a planter on your patio, which are actually members of the genus *Pelargonium*—are excellent for edging pathways, for facing shrubs (particularly in borders), as specimens in rock gardens, and as small-scale lawn substitutes, foundation facers, and soil binders on moderate-sized slopes. They combine well with trees, shrubs, and herbaceous perennials, and in some species, the

Geranium cinereum
'Purple Pillow'

Geranium cinereum
'Splendens'

Geranium macrorrhizum
'Album'

delightfully aromatic foliage perfumes the surrounding air.

Moderate to fast growing; space at a distance equal to two to three times expected mature height. Moist but well-drained, acidic to slightly alkaline soils. Often needs supplemental watering in summer. Full sun or shade depending upon species. Shear back halfway after bloom to promote compactness, or shear midway through the blooming season to initiate another lesser flowering period.

Geranium cinereum
Grayleaf cranesbill

A mound-forming perennial to 4 in. (10 cm) tall by at least twice as wide. Leaves grayish green, divided into five to seven lobes. Flowers pink, 1 in. (2.5 cm) across, with a dark stripe on each petal, summer. Zones 5–7. Pyrenees Mountains.

Geranium macrorrhizum 'Ingwersen's Variety'

'Album', white flowers.

'Ballerina', rose-lavender flowers with purple veins.

'Carol', bright pink flowers with dark purple veins.

'Giuseppii', magenta flowers with dark centers.

'Laurence Flatman', deep green dark blotched foliage, lilac flowers with purple veins.

'Purple Pillow', purple flowers above green foliage.

'Splendens', carmine red flowers.

Geranium macrorrhizum
Bigroot geranium

Valued for its ability to bloom in shade. A robust-growing mat-forming species 12–18 in. (30–45 cm) tall by 2 ft. (60 cm) wide, with thick, fleshy roots. Dies back to just a few inches (centimeters) in winter, but quickly rebounds by spring. Leaves dark green, strongly scented. Flowers magenta, summer. Zones 3–8. Southern Europe.

Drought tolerant. Withstands high temperatures. Sun or shade.

'Album', white petals and pink calyxes.

'Bevan's Variety', 10 in. (25 cm) tall, magenta petals and dark red sepals.

Geranium macrorrhizum 'Variegatum'

'Czakor', deep magenta-pink flowers.

'Ingwersen's Variety', light pink flowers, shiny foliage.

'Lohfelden', compact habit, pale pink flowers, dark pink veins.

'Pindus', similar to 'Czakor' but only about half the height.

'Variegatum', grayish green leaves with irregularly creamy white spots, purplish pink flowers.

Geranium ×*magnificum*

Geranium ×magnificum
Showy geranium

A long-cultivated, fast-spreading sterile hybrid 18–24 in. (45–60 cm) tall by 24 in. (60 cm) wide. Leaves rounded, hairy, deeply divided into five to seven lobes, 2–6 in. (5–15 cm) wide, medium green to silvery green, turning red and yellow in fall. Flowers numerous, saucer shaped, 1½ in. (4 cm) wide and deep violet-blue with blue veins, above the foliage, mid summer. Zones 4–10. *Geranium ibericum* × *G. platypetalum*.

Geranium sanguineum
Bloody cranesbill

A bushy perennial to 12 in. (30 cm) tall, spreading at least 18 in. (45 cm) wide. Leaves deeply divided into five to seven lobes, turning scarlet in fall. Flowers reddish purple to magenta, mid spring to late summer. Zones 3–8. Europe, Asia.

'Alan Bloom', numerous large bright pink flowers.

'Album', white flowers.

'Ankum's Pride', intensely pink flowers with purple veins.

'Cedric Morris', large magenta-pink flowers.

'Holden', 6 in. (15 cm) tall, vibrant pink flowers.

'Max Frei', 8 in. (20 cm) tall, deep magenta flowers, bright autumn foliage.

'Minutum', compact habit, small leaves.

'New Hampshire Purple', 8 in. (20 cm) tall by 24 in. (60 cm) wide, vivid wine-red flowers.

'Shepherd's Warning', many deep magenta-pink flowers.

Var. *striatum* (syn. var. *lancastriense*), large pale pink flowers with dark pink veins.

Grevillea juniperina
Juniper-leaved spider flower

With its unusual foliage and showy clusters of honeysuckle-like flowers that attract hummingbirds, juniper-leaved spider flower functions as a specimen or accent plant, and in mass plantings as general cover. It is excellent along the California coast. Zones 9–11. Australia, Tasmania.

A prostrate, trailing shrub 2–3 ft. (60–90 cm) tall by 6 ft. (1.8 m) wide or more. Leaves prickly, needlelike. Flowers red or yellow.

Geranium sanguineum var. *striatum*

Grevillea juniperina

Moderate to fast growing; space 5–6 ft. (1.5–1.8 m) apart. Any moist but well-drained soil. Tolerates short periods of drought. Full sun or light shade. Prune lightly after flowering to promote compactness.

'**Molonglo**', apricot-colored flowers in winter and spring; frost intolerant.

'**Pink Lady**', pink flowers.

'**Red**', red flowers.

Var. *trinervis*, orange-red flowers in spring and summer.

Grevillea hybrids

Grevilleas comprise a vast group of trees and shrubs from Australia. Because many of the ground-covering types are fairly new to the United States, primarily in California and Arizona, little is known about them.

Austraflora series, a mix of yellow, red, and pink flowers, often with coppery or bronzy gold new growth.

'**Bronze Rambler**', deeply divided, sharply pointed oaklike foliage, bronzy red when young becoming bronze tinged in cooler weather

'**Noell**', rose-red and white flowers, green needlelike foliage, frost tolerant.

'**Poorinda Royal Mantle**', young leaves red, mature leaves dark green, flowers dark red, fast growing, superb for cascading over the edge of boulders and retaining walls, frost intolerant.

'**White Wings**', fast spreading, white flowers in winter and spring, frost intolerant.

HEDERA
Ivy

Among the most versatile, useful, and reliable woody ground covers, ivies are magnificent for their shiny evergreen foliage, which comes in countless variations. In the juvenile stage, the plants are vinelike, climbing or trailing, nonflowering, with three- or five-lobed leaves. In the

Grevillea 'White Wings'

adult form, ivies produce unlobed, darker green foliage and small white to greenish flowers followed by black capsules. Normally, ivies only make the transition from juvenile to adult form when their branches have climbed upward as far as they can go and no longer find support. At this point the new growth displays the characteristics of the adult stage.

Juvenile forms make good ground covers, reaching 2–6 in. (5–15 cm) high when unsupported and spreading indefinitely. They are best in moderate or large areas and substitute well for turf grass. Their performance in the poor soil along building foundations is admirable. Planted next to ledges and allowed to trail over or near walls that they can climb, they introduce an intriguing cascading or vertical dimension. On steep slopes and banks they are among the most successful soil stabilizers. Regardless of their use, they project an image of aristocracy with their rich evergreen lushness.

Slow growing initially, then faster as plants mature; space 10–14 in. (25–35 cm) apart, 6–10 in. (15–25 cm) apart if slow growing. Best in rich, acidic loam but tolerates heavier or lighter, more alkaline soils. Drought tolerant but best when watered thoroughly once or twice per week during the summer. Full sun to dense shade. Clip back stems as they outgrow their bounds.

Hedera canariensis
Canary Island ivy, Algerian ivy
A staple ground cover of the California coast. Juvenile leaves 6 in. (15 cm) long and wide, divided into three to seven lobes, heart shaped, light to medium green, shiny, smooth. Zones 8–10. Canary Islands, North Africa.

'**Azorica**', vigorous habit.

'**Margino-maculata**', cream-colored leaf margins flecked or spotted with green.

'**Ravensholst**', vigorous habit, leaves larger than those of the species.

Hedera canariensis

'Souvenir de Marengo' (syns. 'Variegata', 'Gloire de Marengo'), leaf margins silvery white.

'Striata', leaf margins green, midsection streaked light green to ivory.

Hedera colchica
Persian ivy, fragrant ivy

Leaves heart shaped, slightly lobed, thick, leathery, to 10 in. (25 cm) long, dark dull green, smelling of celery when crushed. Zones 5–10. Asia, southwestern Europe.

'Dentata', shiny green, finely toothed leaves.

'Dentata Variegata', leaf edges irregularly variegated with creamy yellow.

'Sulfur Heart' (syns. 'Gold Leaf', 'Paddy's Pride'), leaves light green with yellowish central variegation.

Hedera helix
English ivy

Beyond compare in popularity. The most widely cultivated ivy in North America. Juvenile leaves composed of three to five lobes, triangular to oval, 2–3 in. (5.0–7.5 cm) long, smooth, dark shiny green with whitish to cream-colored veins. Zones 5–9; a few cultivars only to Zone 7. Europe.

'Baltica', smaller leaves with white veins, Zone 5.

'Brocamp', light green, willow-shaped leaves, Zone 6.

'Buttercup', leaves yellow in youth if grown in the sun, otherwise green, Zone 6.

'Caecilia', creamy white wavy leaf margins, Zone 6.

'California Fan', small light green, fan-shaped leaves, Zone 7.

'California Gold', leaves mottled green and butterscotch, Zone 6.

'Chester', broad green and gray-green leaves edged in creamy white, Zone 6 or 7.

'Duckfoot', small leaves that resemble a duck's foot, Zone 6.

'Flamenco', twisted and curled leaves, Zone 6.

'Galaxy', star-shaped, medium green leaves, Zone 6.

'Glacier', small green leaves with pinkish and creamy white edges, Zone 7.

'Golden Ingot', bright yellow leaves edged with dark green and decorated in the center with splashes of green and gray, Zone 6.

'Goldheart', small, green leaves with yellow and cream centers, Zone 7.

'Hahn's' (syn. 'Hahn's Self-Branching'), small, light green leaves, Zone 7.

'Jubilee', vigorous growth, miniature leaves, Zone 6.

'Lady Frances', miniature gray-green foliage with white variegation, Zone 6 or 7.

'Midget', compact habit, densely set green leaves, Zone 6.

Hedera colchica 'Dentata Variegata'

Hedera colchica 'Sulfur Heart'

Hedera helix

Hedera helix 'Baltica'

Hedera helix 'Thorndale'

'**Needlepoint**', popular in the southern United States, leaves smaller with a long, narrow center lobe, Zone 7.

'**Pedata**', bird's foot ivy, small leaves with five sharp lobes, Zone 7.

'**Pixie**', crinkle-edged, deep green, deeply lobed leaves with white veins, Zone 6.

'**Teardrop**', thick leathery deep green teardrop-shaped foliage with white veins, Zone 6.

'**Thorndale**', leaves slightly smaller than the species with pronounced central lobe and white veins, Zone 5.

'**Walthamensis**', leaves 1 in. (2.5 cm) wide, dark green, turning blackish green in winter, Zone 5.

'**Woerner**', vigorous habit, dull green leaves turning purple in winter, Zone 5.

Helianthemum hybrids
Sun rose

Best as a specimen in a rock garden, overhanging a stone retaining wall, or edging paths and walkways, sun rose also is a colorful facing when massed on a small scale. Zones 5–7 in warm humid climates; up to Zone 9 along the coast.

A low-growing, trailing, woody shrublet 6–12 in. (15–30 cm) tall, spreading to 3 ft. (90 cm) across. Leaves oval to linear, evergreen, to 2 in. (5 cm) long by ¼ in. (6 mm) wide, gray-green, unassuming. Flowers large, brightly colored, numerous, 1 in. (2.5 cm) wide, pink or dusty rose fading to apricot, produced in quantity but only lasting one day, early to mid summer.

Slow growing until the roots become well established, then moderate growing; space 24–30 in. (60–75 cm) apart. Gravelly, slightly alkaline, well-drained soil. Very drought tolerant, but welcomes an occasional watering in summer. Full sun; light shade in warm climates. Lightly shear when plants become too lanky or begin to wander outside of their designated territories.

'**Amy Baring**', buttercup yellow flowers.

'**Ben Afflick**', golden yellow flowers with orange centers.

'**Ben Nevis**', deep yellow flowers with bronzy red centers.

Helianthemum 'Wisley Pink'

Helleborus ×*hybridus*

Helleborus ×*hybridus* 'Red Lady'

'Cerise Queen', double red flowers.

'Cheviot', apricot-colored flowers.

'Fireball' (syn. 'Mrs. C. W. Earle'), dark red single flowers.

'Henfield Brilliant', bright coppery yellow flowers.

'Jubilee', double yellow flowers.

'Orange Surprise', golden orange flowers with dark orange centers, olive green leaves.

'Raspberry Ripple', raspberry red flowers.

Rose Queen (syn. 'Rosa Königin'), rose-pink double flowers.

'Watergate Rose', rose-crimson flowers with orangish centers.

'Wisley Pink', pink flowers.

'Wisley Primrose', light yellow flowers.

'Wisley White', white flowers.

Helleborus ×hybridus
Hybrid Lenten rose

Under this heading is an array of outstanding selections derived from crosses which involve *H. niger*, *H. orientalis* (Lenten rose), and cultivars of both species. Finally, in North America they have come into their heyday and are valued for their early-season flowering (often blooming through the snow) and for their rugged, coarse-textured, leathery, shiny green foliage that remains attractive year-round. Christmas rose is ideally suited for use on a small to moderate scale in naturalistic woodland landscapes and is best employed on sloping ground to increase the visibility of its charming flowers and as edging for a sidewalk or garden path. It combines well with showy bulbs, woodland lilies, and hostas. Zones 3–8. Europe.

A stemless herb 12–18 in. (30–45 cm) tall, spreading about the same across. Leaves erect, dark, shiny green, edged with shallow teeth. Flowers whitish with pink tinges, in late winter, occasionally flowering on Christmas Day.

Slow growing; space 14–18 in. (35–45 cm) apart. Well-drained, rich, alkaline soil. Moderately drought tolerant. Light to moderate shade. All parts of the plant are poisonous, and in some individuals, skin contact with the sap can cause dermatitis.

'Blue Lady', bluish purple flowers.

Ivory Prince (syn. 'Walhelivory'), ivory flowers flushed pink and streaked with green and rose.

'Mrs. Betty Ranicar', double white flowers.

Pine Knot Doubles, a mix of double pink, rose, purple, white, and yellow flowers, including those with rounded as well as pointed petals.

'Pink Lady', pink and rose flowers.

'Red Lady', rich red flowers with deeper centers.

Royal Heritage Strain, a mix of purple, red, rose-pink, yellow, and pale green to nearly black flowers.

'White Lady Spotted', creamy chartreuse flowers with deep red markings.

Hemerocallis hybrids
Hybrid daylilies

Daylilies are among the most useful ground covers for small through large areas. Nearly indestructible, they are excellent as accent and specimen plants. Placed atop a retaining wall, on sloping terrain, or in beds paralleling steps brings them up to eye level where they can be appreciated to the fullest. Along walkways they are exceptional edgings and at building entrances they present a colorful, welcoming appearance. Frequently they are employed as foundation plants or as erosion-controlling soil binders at the edge of a pond or stream. Zones 3–9.

Leaves are broad straplike blades, evergreen or deciduous, 6–14 in. (15–35 cm) long on short varieties, up to 2 or 3 ft. (60–90 cm) long on some of the taller forms, light to medium green to grayish or even blue-green, often arching over. Flowers trumpet shaped, above the mass of leaves, 16–30 in. (40–75 cm) tall by 3–5 in. (7.5–13.0 cm) wide, opening during the day, lasting only a day, colored yellow, orange, pink, red, or purplish, and all combinations, sometimes fragrant, and sometimes with ruffled or brocaded edges.

Moderate to fast growing; space 14–30 in. (35–75 cm) apart. Moist, rich, acidic, well-drained loam. Drought tolerant, but an occasional deep watering throughout the flowering season results in maximum flower production.

Hemerocallis 'Chicago Apache'

Hemerocallis 'Happy Returns'

Hemerocallis 'Stella de Oro'

Full sun to moderate shade; dark-flowered varieties are best in afternoon shade.

In the descriptions that follow the bloom season designates the onset of flowering. Most cultivars display a main bloom period of two to six weeks. Rebloomers may rest for a short while (which may be virtually imperceptible or three to four weeks) after the primary bloom season, then continue to produce flowers. Although the second period of flowering is not as prolific as the first, it may last for much of the remainder of the growing season. All the plants listed here have won awards.

'Always Afternoon', early season, repeat blooming, flowers with medium mauve-purple centers and green throats; semievergreen.

'Catherine Woodbury', flowers soft salmon-pink.

'Chicago Apache', flowers scarlet red.

'Custard Candy', flowers creamy yellow with maroon centers and picotee edges, borne in summer, repeating sporadically until fall.

'Gentle Shepherd', flowers creamy white with a heavy substance.

'Happy Returns', flowers lemon yellow, reblooming, extremely popular.

'Janice Brown', early to midseason, flowers bright pink with rose-pink centers and green throats; semievergreen.

'Joan Senlor', early to midseason, repeat blooming, flowers 6 in. (15 cm) wide, near white with lime-green throats; evergreen.

'Little Grapette', flowers 2 in. (5 cm) wide, grape purple with yellow centers and a heavy substance.

'Mardi Gras Parade', flowers bright rose-lavender with rich, ruby red centers.

'Mary Todd', early season, flowers 6 in. (15 cm) wide, buff-yellow; semievergreen.

'Moonlit Masquerade', flowers pale cream to near white with purple centers.

'Pardon Me', midseason, flowers 2¾ in. (7 cm) wide, bright red with yellow-green throats; deciduous.

'Primal Scream', flowers bright tangerine and curry-colored with backwards bending ruffled petals.

'Stella de Oro', the most popular daylily in the United States, early to late season, repeat blooming, flowers 2¾ in. (7 cm) wide, golden; deciduous.

'Strawberry Candy', repeat blooming, flowers bright strawberry-pink with rose centers and red spots about their edges; semievergreen.

'Sue Rothbauer', flowers 6½ in. (16 cm) wide, cherry rose-pink with yellowish green centers, reblooming.

'Summer Wine', flowers rich wine red with yellow centers.

Herniaria glabra
Rupturewort

Hemerocallis 'Sue Rothbauer'

With nearly unnoticeable flowers and fruit, rupturewort might be considered unusable. But this boring groundcover is functional. It dutifully smothers the ground and excludes weeds. Rupturewort is useful between stepping stones and as a turf substitute in smaller areas, and provides a pleasant mosslike cover. Colorful bulbs and herbaceous perennials can be interplanted to add interest. Zones 5–10. Europe, northern and western Asia, Africa, Turkey.

A perennial 2–3 in. (5.0–7.5 cm) tall. Leaves evergreen, simple, oval to elliptic, ⅛–⅜ in. (3–9 mm) long by ⅛ in. (3 mm) wide, bright shiny green, turning bronzy in winter. Flowers tiny, greenish yellow, mid summer.

Hemerocallis 'Summer Wine'

Slow to moderate; space 6–12 in. (15–30 cm) apart. Well-drained neutral to acidic soil. Water during the summer. Full sun to light shade. Trim back stems as they outgrow their bounds.

'Green Carpet', ½–1in. (12–25 mm) tall.

'Sea Foam', green leaves edged with creamy white; full sun.

Heuchera sanguinea
Coral bells

One of the most prized native North American herbs, coral bells is typically used in small to moderate plantings as a general cover or as a facing to buildings, trees, and woodland borders. Not too rambunctious, it is also excellent as an edging to garden paths and sidewalks and

Herniaria glabra 'Sea Foam'

Heuchera 'Amber Waves' (photo by Tony Avent)

Heuchera 'Peach Flambe' (photo by Tony Avent)

border plantings of perennials. Zones 3–9. Mexico, Arizona.

A clump-forming herb 12–18 in. (30–45 cm) tall, spreading 2–3 ft. (60–90 cm) across. Leaves evergreen, roundish to heart shaped, dark to grayish green (with reddish winter pigmentation), 1–2 in. (2.5–5.0 cm) long and wide. Flowers red to pink, bell shaped, above the leaves, mid spring through early fall.

Slow growing; space 12–14 in. (30–35 cm) apart. Well-drained, slightly acidic loam but tolerates neutral and slightly alkaline soil. Fairly drought tolerant. Full sun to light shade. Prune off the flower stalks at the end of the blooming season.

The parentage of many cultivars is complex. Some of the most common plants, listed here, are hybrid selections of various species and cultivars.

'Amber Waves', ruffled amber-gold foliage, cream flowers.

'Amethyst Myst', blackish purple, silvery blue overlaid foliage, creamy white flowers.

'Black Beauty', deep reddish purple, glossy, ruffled foliage, white flowers.

'Champagne Bubbles', bright glossy green foliage, an "effervescent" show of white to rose-red flowers.

'Cherries Jubilee', dusty bronze-purple foliage, bright cherry red flowers.

'Ebony and Ivory', deep purple ruffled foliage, ivory flowers.

'Frosted Violet', deep plum-purple, silvery overlaid foliage, pink flowers.

'Green Spice', green leaves overlaid with silver and decorated with deep beet-red veins, cream-colored flowers.

'Lime Ricky', shockingly lime-green ruffled foliage, pure white flowers.

'Marmalade', shiny amber to rose-orange foliage, reddish brown flowers.

Heuchera 'Silver Scrolls' (photo by Tony Avent)

'**Obsidian**', deep purplish leaves appearing almost black, cream-colored flowers.

'**Peach Flambe**', bright peach-colored leaves becoming red infused in winter, white flowers.

'**Purple Petticoats**', deep purple ruffled foliage, cream-colored flowers.

'**Raspberry Ice**', plum purple foliage overlaid in metallic silver, deep rose-pink flowers.

'**Regina**', bronze-purple foliage overlaid in silvery gray, light pink flowers.

'**Silver Scrolls**', deep grape purple foliage overlaid in silvery gray, greenish cream flowers.

'**Venus**', large maple-shaped silvery leaves with purple veins.

Hosta cultivars
Hosta, plaintain lily

The endlessly useful hostas rank among the most popular herbaceous ground covers. They require almost no maintenance, become larger and more valuable each year, offer food to bees and hummingbirds, and enrich the soil as they die back to the earth each fall. They are widely employed for edging walks and perennial borders and as accents in ornamental beds of shrubs and low-growing trees. A dramatic lush appearance is obtained when masses of hostas are planted as bank coverings or facings to trees and foundations, and a single large specimen is always very attention getting. Hostas combine well with astilbes, ferns, lilies, spring-flowering bulbs, and countless varieties of deciduous and evergreen trees and shrubs. Zones 3–9. China, Korea, Japan.

A clump-forming perennial from a couple of inches (centimeters) tall to more than 3 ft. (90 cm), spreading one to five times its height. Leaves deciduous, long and narrow to short and broad, tiny to huge, smooth to corrugated, oval or heart shaped, often conspicuously

Hosta 'Blue Angel'

Hosta 'Frosted Jade'

Hosta 'Gold Standard'

veined. Flowers trumpet shaped, white to purple, sometimes fragrant, usually elevated above the foliage.

Moderate growing, except for some slow-growing dwarf forms; space at a distance equal to the expected mature spread, usually 12–36 in. (30–90 cm). Moist but well-drained, acidic, sandy or light loamy soils. Protect from wind. Light to dense shade; full sun okay in cool climates with high humidity.

'Blue Angel', 30 in. (75 cm) tall by 6 ft. (1.8 m) wide, huge blue heavy-textured leaves, white flowers in mid summer.

'Brim Cup', less than 10 in. (25 cm) tall, seersuckered rich green foliage edged in white, light blue flowers.

'Cherry Berry', 12 in. (30 cm) tall, unique narrow leaves with a white center and a green edge, purplish red scapes, lavender-purple flowers in mid to late summer.

'Daybreak', to 2 ft. (60 cm) tall, long heart-shaped iridescent golden yellow foliage with deep veins, fragrant lavender flowers in summer.

'Dream Weaver', 18 in. (45 cm) tall, large creamy yellow foliage with a heavy margin of blue-green, white flowers.

'Fragrant Blue', to 12 in. (30 cm) tall, frosty blue foliage, highly fragrant light lavender flowers.

'Francis Williams', giant blue-green, leathery, corrugated leaves broadly edged in yellow, white flowers.

'Frosted Jade', 30 in. (75 cm) tall, magnificent heart-shaped frosty bluish green foliage edged and streaked with ivory white.

'Gold Standard', 15 in. (38 cm) tall, deep green leaves with bright yellow centers, lavender flowers.

'Golden Tiara', 15 in. (38 cm) tall, small, heart-shaped, medium green leaves edged in chartreuse, deep lavender flowers.

'Great Expectations', slowly reaching 20 in. (50 cm) tall by 2 ft. (60 cm) across, gold leaves irregularly edged with blue-green, white flowers.

'Hadspen Blue', one of the finest blue-leaved forms, 12 in. (30 cm) tall, blue-lavender flowers.

'Halcyon', 16 in. (40 cm) tall by 32 in. (80 cm) wide, deep bluish green leaves, lavender flowers.

'June', blue- and green-edged leaves with golden centers often bleaching to creamy white in sun.

'Krossa Regal', to 3 ft. (90 cm) tall, frosty blue upright leaves, lavender flowers.

'Patriot', 12 in. (30 cm) tall by 30 in. (75 cm) wide, dark green leaves broadly edged in bright white.

'Piedmont Gold', 18 in. (45 cm) tall, golden leaves, white flowers.

'Praying Hands', 14–18 in. (35–45 cm) tall, unusual dark green narrow leaves edged in gold and heavily incurled, lavender flowers.

'Regal Splendor', 3 ft. (90 cm) tall, frosty blue-green leaves neatly edged in creamy yellow.

'Royal Standard', 26 in. (65 cm) tall, classic green leaves, very fragrant snow white flowers.

Hosta 'Krossa Regal'

Hosta 'Sagae'

Hosta 'Piedmont Gold'

'Sagae', 28 in. (70 cm) tall, huge, wavy-edged, frosty blue-green leaves irregularly edged in creamy yellow, fragrant lavender flowers.

'Striptease', 20 in. (50 cm) tall, dark green leaves with a narrow cream stripe.

'Sum and Substance', 20 in. (50 cm) tall by 6 ft. (1.8 m) wide, extraordinary selection with giant rounded chartreuse leaves, pale lavender flowers.

Houttuynia cordata 'Variegata'
Chameleon houttuynia

This unusual herb functions well in small to large areas and must be either given room to spread or surrounded by a deep edging or sidewalk. Chameleon houttuynia is used as a facing to shrubs with dark green leaves. Because it withstands high moisture, it is well suited to stabilize the soil around ponds and streams. It is sometimes grown in containers placed directly in the water. Zones 4–8.

A tenacious rhizomatous perennial 12–15 in. (30–38 cm) tall, spreading indefinitely. Leaves deciduous, simple, oval to heart shaped, 2–3 in. (5.0–7.5 cm) long by 1½ in. (4 cm) wide, smelling of citrus, variegated yellow, green, pale green, gray, cream, and scarlet. Flowers tiny, yellowish, in spikes subtended by four white petal-like bracts, reminiscent of dogwood, mid spring.

Moderate to fast growing; space 8–10 in. (20–25 cm) apart. Any constantly moist or wet soil. Full sun to moderate shade.

HYPERICUM
Saint John's-wort

The tall representatives of the genus may be better known, but some of the slower-growing, more refined, low-shrubby forms can be used as ground covers for walk and driveway edging. In addition, several low, trailing, subshrubby forms excel as ground covers. Of great usefulness on medium to large slopes, they are exceptional for their dense network of erosion-controlling roots and rhizomes, dark green semisucculent foliage, assertive spreading qualities, and extraordinary bright yellow flowers.

Houttuynia cordata 'Variegata'

Moderate growing; space 30–36 in. (75–90 cm) apart. Well-drained, fertile, acidic loam. Drought tolerant for short periods. Full sun to partial shade.

Hypericum calycinum
Creeping Saint John's-wort

A shrub 12–18 in. (30–45 cm) tall, spreading indefinitely. Leaves aromatic, semievergreen, oval to oblong, to 4 in. (10 cm) long by 1 in. (2.5 cm) wide, medium to dark green above, bluish green below, becoming purplish in fall. Flowers numerous, cheerful, yellow, 3 in. (7.5 cm) wide, early summer to early fall. Zones 5–10. Southeastern Europe, Turkey.

HYPERICUM

Hypericum calycinum

Hypericum 'Hidcote'

Hypericum 'Hidcote'

A more or less upright shrub 18–24 in. (45–60 cm) tall in cold climates and to 3 ft. (90 cm) tall in warm climates, broadly spreading as wide as it is tall. Leaves semievergreen, oval to narrowly oblong, medium green. Flowers yellow, 2 in. (5 cm) in diameter, early summer to mid fall. Zones 5–9. *Hypericum* ×*cyanthiflorum* 'Gold Cup' × *H. calycinum*, or *H. forrestii* × *H. calycinum*.

Iberis sempervirens
Evergreen candytuft

"Tidy" is an appropriate adjective for evergreen candytuft. It is an effective edging along walkways and terrace margins, and also performs exceptionally well as a specimen in rock gardens or as a small-scale general cover, particularly in beds that are slightly elevated and surrounded by a rocky border. Candytuft can be used as facing in front of building foundations, ornaments, and dwarf shrubs, especially those with bronze leaves. Zones 5–7. Europe, Asia.

A low-growing, semiwoody, densely growing, upright subshrub 12 in. (30 cm) tall, spreading 3–4 ft. (90–120 cm) across. Leaves deep shiny green, linear, 1–1½ in. (2.5–4.0 cm) long by ⅛–¼ in. (3–6 mm) wide. Flowers white, ⅜ in. (9 cm) wide, in clusters 2 in. (5 cm) across, late spring or early summer. Fruit a flattened, almost podlike seed.

Slow growing; space 18–24 in. (45–60 cm) apart. Any well-drained soil. Drought tolerant, but an occasional deep watering is required during extended periods of hot, dry weather. Full sun.

'Alexander's White', compact habit, early bloom.

'Autumn Beauty', compact habit, vibrant white flowers in early spring and again in fall.

'Kingwood Compact', compact habit, heavy blooming, 8 in. (20 cm) tall.

Little Gem (syn. 'Weisser Zwerg'), compact habit, 5 in. (13 cm) tall by 8–10 in. (20–25 cm) wide.

'October Glory', blooming in spring and fall.

Iberis sempervirens 'Snowflake'

'Purity', flowers more numerous and longer lasting.

'Pygmaea', low-growing, horizontally spreading.

'Snow Mantle', 15 in. (38 cm) tall, dark green leaves, pure white flowers.

'Snowflake', larger waxy white flowers, broader and darker green leaves.

Ilex crenata
Japanese holly, box-leaved holly

Japanese holly is best used for edging walkways and driveways, as a dwarf hedge, and as a foundation facer. Zones 6–9. Japan.

A mounding holly 2–3 ft. (60–90 cm) tall by 3–6 ft. (90–180 cm) wide. Leaves evergreen, densely set, elliptic, oblong, or narrowly oval, 1¼ in. (3 cm) long by ⅝ in. (15 mm) wide, edged with rounded or pointed teeth, shiny, smooth, dark green above, pale green below. Flowers dull white, small, late spring to early summer. Fruit a round black berry ¼ in. (6 mm) in diameter.

Slow growing; space at a distance of 75 percent of the expected mature width. Well-drained, slightly acidic loam. Drought tolerant but benefits from supplemental watering in summer. Full sun or light shade. Lightly shear in spring.

'Angelica', low spreading habit, narrow leaves.

'Border Gem', dense low growing habit, deep green foliage.

'Compacta', globe-shaped habit.

'Convexa', like 'Compacta' but with cup-shaped leaves.

'Helleri', compact, mound-forming.

'Hetzii', like 'Compacta' but with larger leaves and a faster rate of growth.

'Kingsville Green Cushion', 8 in. (20 cm) tall by 3 ft. (90 cm) wide.

Indigofera kirilowii
Kirilow indigo

With its soft-textured pealike foliage, kirilow indigo makes an attractive general cover or soil stabilizer in moderate to large areas. Zones 5–7. Northern China, Korea.

A low-growing, dense, suckering shrub 3 ft. (90 cm) tall. Leaves semievergreen, 1¼–1¾ in.

(30–45 mm) long, composed of three to five pairs of elliptic to oval leaflets. Flowers pealike, bright rose-colored, ¾ in. (2 cm) long, mid summer.

Fast growing; space 3–4 ft. (90–120 cm) apart. Moist but well-drained, acidic to slightly alkaline loam. Full sun. Cut plants back to the living wood in spring, or mow them to the ground shortly after winter.

'Alba', white flowers.

IRIS

Irises are heralded for their marvelous flowers (characterized by three upright petals, or standards, and three drooping sepals, or falls) and attractive sword-shaped foliage. Normally planted in small clumps, irises may not be what most people think of as ground covers; however, in mass plantings they perform admirably, spreading either by creeping rhizomes or offsets of bulbous crowns.

Along walks and drives, or a mixed herbaceous border, an edging of irises is very attractive. Many irises tolerate wet soil and therefore are useful near streams, ponds, and reflecting pools. On the sloping sides of a drainage ditch, irises bind soil beautifully, and as a compact clump in the rock garden they can infuse a much-needed vertical dimension.

Slow to moderate growing. Moist to slightly wet, fertile loam. Drought tolerant. Full sun to moderate shade. Cut foliage to ground level each fall to encourage compact growth and good health.

Iris cristata
Dwarf crested iris

A mat-forming iris seldom exceeding 7 in. (18 cm) tall, spreading indefinitely. Leaves deciduous, medium green, 4–9 in. (11–23 cm) long, sword shaped. Flowers small, only 1–2½ in. (2.5–6.0 cm) wide, pale lilac with white or yellow crests on the falls, spring. Zones 3–9. Maryland to Michigan, south to Georgia and Missouri

Space plants 10–14 in. (25–35 cm) apart.

'Alba', white flowers.

'Navy Blue Gem', deep blue, almost purple flowers.

Ilex crenata 'Helleri'

Indigofera kirilowii

Iris cristata

Iris cristata 'Alba'

Iris cristata 'Navy Blue Gem'

Iris pseudacorus 'Flore-Plena'

Iris ensata
Japanese iris

A rhizomatous iris about 3 ft. (90 cm) tall. Leaves bright green, prominently ribbed. Flowers with reddish purple falls, yellow centers, dark veins, and white upright standards, early to mid summer. Zones 5–10. Manchuria, Korea, Japan.

Moist, acidic soil, drier in fall and winter. Full sun.

'**August Emperor**', double purple flowers edged in white and blue.

'**Crystal Halo**', reddish purple flowers with white edges.

'**Ebb and Flow**', medium blue flowers with violet edges and dark blue centers.

'**Frilled Enchantment**', white, ruffled flowers with rose-red edges.

'**Frosted Pyramid**', pure white, ruffled flowers resembling peonies.

'**Oriental Eyes**', flowers with purple falls, violet centers, and light violet edges.

'**Over The Waves**', magnificent double, reddish purple flowers with white veins.

'**Pin Stripe**', double white flowers with blue veins.

'**Reign of Glory**', flowers with soft purple falls and white veins.

'**Sensation**', double rich, violet-blue flowers with yellow signals.

'**Variegata**', leaves with lovely white and green variegation.

'**Wine Ruffles**', double, deep grape purple flowers 8 in. (20 cm) wide.

Iris pseudacorus
Yellow flag

An inhabitant of moist, marshy areas that is excellent at the bank of a pond or as a specimen next to a waterfall. Leaves massive, grasslike, medium green, to 4 ft. (1.2 m) tall. Flowers yellow, mid spring to mid summer. Zones 5–9. Europe, Siberia, Caucasus, western Asia, North Africa; naturalized in North America.

Tolerates saturated soils.

'**Alba**', pale, creamy yellow flowers.

'**Flore-Plena**', double flowers.

'**Nana**', about half the size of the species.

Iris ensata 'Variegata'

Iris pseudacorus
'Roy Davidson'

Isotoma fluviatilis

'Roy Davidson', yellow petals marked with brown.

Isotoma fluviatilis
Blue-star creeper

Blue-star creeper, sometimes listed as *Laurentia fluviatilis* or *Pratia pedunculata*, is typically used as a general cover for small to moderate areas and as a filler between stepping stones. Zones 6–10. Southern Australia, Tasmania, New Zealand.

A low-growing, mat-forming herb 2–5 in. (5–13 cm) tall, spreading indefinitely. Leaves evergreen, oval, ½ in. (12 mm) long, medium dull green above, purplish below, edged with small lobes and tiny hairs. Flowers light blue or whitish, ⅜ in. (9 mm) wide, irregularly star shaped, late spring and intermittently throughout summer.

Moderate to fast growing; space 8–12 in. (20–30 cm) apart. Most soils. Needs regular watering in summer. Light shade. Trim back plants as they outgrow their bounds.

Jasminum nudiflorum
Winter jasmine

Winter jasmine produces numerous showy, pleasantly scented flowers, tends to be somewhat lax or casual in appearance, and is normally best when its trailing branches can cascade over the edge of something. Hillsides, planters, terraces, and atop retaining walls are all good sites for jasmine. Zones 6–10. China.

Jasminum nudiflorum

A relatively woody, vinelike plant with a distinctive scrambling habit, 2–3 ft. (60–90 cm) tall, spreading 4–7 ft. (1.2–2.1 m) wide. Leaves deciduous, composed of three leaflets, each shiny green, oval to oblong-oval, 1¼ in. (3 cm) long by ½ in. (12 mm) wide. Flowers bright yellow, trumpet shaped, 2 in. (5 cm) long by 1 in. (2.5 cm) wide, early spring before the leaves appear. Fruit a black berry, sparse, savored by songbirds.

Fast growing; space 3–4 ft. (90–120 cm) apart. Most well-drained, acidic soils. Moderately drought tolerant, but benefits from an occasional deep watering in summer. Full sun to moderate shade. Cut plants to within 6 in. (15 cm) of the ground every few years to neaten appearance and rejuvenate growth.

'Aureum', yellow-blotched foliage.

'Nanum', more compact and slower growing.

'Variegatum', gray-green leaves edged in white, slower growing.

JUNIPERUS
Juniper

Ground-covering junipers are some of the finest, most durable, drought-resistant, low-maintenance plants available. They are excellent when mass planted on a moderate to large scale as turf substitutes and as facers for foundations and open shrubs and trees. They are superior for erosion control on slopes of light to moderate incline and are graceful next to a rock ledge over which their branches can hang.

Only a few species fit the description of ground cover and are described here. Other, more upright species have produced horizontally growing cultivars that make effective ground covers.

Well-drained, neutral to acidic loam. Very drought tolerant. Protect from excessive humidity. Full sun. Cut off the branch tips as plants outgrow their designated bounds.

Juniperus conferta

Juniperus conferta
Shore juniper

A dense, horizontal, wide-spreading shrub 12–18 in. (30–45 cm) tall, spreading to over 6 ft. (1.8 m) wide. Leaves needlelike, evergreen, ¼–⅝ in. (6–15 mm) long by 1/16 in. (less than 2 mm) wide, prickly. Zones 6–8. Japan, along the coast.

Slow growing; space 3–4 ft. (90–120 cm) apart.

'Akebono', creamy yellow new growth turning to green with age.

'Blue Lagoon', lower growing with blue-green foliage.

'Blue Mist', 12 in. (30 cm) tall by 8 ft. (2.4 m) wide with blue foliage.

'Blue Pacific', 6–12 in. (15–30 cm) high with blue-green needles.

'Boulevard', blue-green needles.

'Compacta', more compact and horizontal than the species.

'Emerald Sea', 6–12 in. (15–30 cm) tall, with a gray-green band on emerald green needles that become yellow-green in winter.

'Variegata', bluish green foliage mixed with yellow.

Juniperus horizontalis
Creeping juniper, horizontal juniper

A horizontal, mat forming shrub 1–2 ft. (30–60 cm) tall by 4–6 ft. (1.2–1.8 m) wide. Leaves evergreen, blue-green to steel green, often turning purple during fall, awl shaped when juvenile, scalelike when adult. Fruit roundish blue. Zones 2–9. Nova Scotia to British Columbia.

Slow to moderate growing; space 3–4 ft. (90–120 cm) apart.

'Aurea', golden yellow new foliage.

'Bar Harbor', steel blue, turning purplish blue in fall.

'Blue Chip', silvery blue foliage, mound-forming, 8–10 in. (20–25 cm) tall.

'Emerald Spreader', feathery, emerald green foliage, very low growing.

'Jade Spreader', compact, very low growing, with jade green foliage.

'Mother Lode', bright yellow foliage becoming yellow-orange and plum-tinged during winter.

Juniperus horizontalis 'Blue Chip'

Juniperus horizontalis 'Wiltonii'

Juniperus procumbens
'Nana'

Lamiastrum galeobdolon
'Herman's Pride'

Lamium maculatum
'Orchid Frost'

'Pancake', only 2 in. (5 cm) tall and spreading more than 30 in. (75 cm) wide.

'Turquoise Spreader', a low, spreading habit and dense, turquoise-green feathery foliage.

'Variegata', blue-green with branchlets tipped creamy white, vigorous and low growing.

'Wiltonii' (syn. 'Blue Rug'), probably the most popular cultivar, silvery blue foliage sometimes with a hint of purple in winter.

Juniperus procumbens
Japanese garden juniper

A trailing shrub 10–12 in. (25–30 cm) tall, spreading over 10 ft. (3 m) across. Leaves sharply pointed, needlelike, 1/3 in. (8 mm) long. Fruit rare in cultivation. Zones 5–9. Japan.

Slow growing; space 3–4 ft. (90–120 cm) apart.

'Green Mound', vibrant light green foliage.

'Nana', seldom more than 4 in. (10 cm) tall, eventually reaching 6–8 ft. (1.8–2.4 m) wide, with blue-green foliage becoming slightly purplish in winter.

'Variegata', leaves variegated creamy white and green.

Lamiastrum galeobdolon
Yellow archangel

Excellent in large open areas and especially on sloping ground and terraced hillsides, yellow archangel is also suitable for elevated planters. Zones 4–9. Western Europe to Iran.

An almost vinelike, trailing species. Leaves evergreen, oval to nearly round, to 3 in. (7.5 cm) long, covered with sparse hairs, toothed along the edges, aromatic when crushed. Flowers yellow, 1/2–3/4 in. (12–20 mm) long, late spring.

Fast growing; space 12–18 in. (30–45 cm) apart. Rich, fertile, acidic loam; slower growing in infertile sandy soils. Occasional summer watering may be necessary. Light to moderate shade; full sun if soil is rich and if ample water is provided.

'Herman's Pride', clump-forming, nontrailing, leaves with intensely silver and green variegation (at least during spring), sometimes fading to a rather unattractive mottled pattern during the heat of summer, best in a cool shady location as an accent or specimen.

'Variegatum', leaves silvery and green with a blood-red to purplish center splotch in autumn, excellent in the shade surrounding tree trunks or in mass plantings in shady woodland borders.

Lamium maculatum
Spotted dead nettle

Charming and colorful, spotted dead nettle is typically used on a small scale. Its variegated foliage contrasts nicely with the darker leaves of other plants, making it an excellent facing for hedges or grouped plantings. Zones 3–8. Europe.

A clump-forming, horizontally spreading herb 6–8 in. (15–20 cm) tall by 12–16 in. (30–40 cm) across. Leaves evergreen, crinkled, edged with rounded teeth, oval to heart shaped, 1 in. (2.5 cm) long by 1/2 in. (12 mm) wide, green with a silvery gray splash in the center, unpleasantly scented when rubbed, bruised, or crushed. Flowers lavender, 5/8 in. (15 mm) long, spring and early summer, often with fall rebloom.

Moderate growing; space 6–10 in. (15–25 cm) apart. Moist but well-drained, rich acidic loam. Full sun to moderate shade; more shade further south. Sometimes mowed after flowering to keep plantings rejuvenated and vibrant.

'Aureum', leaves yellowish with a whitish blotch along the midrib, less aggressive, best in shade.

'Beacon Silver', radiant silver leaves surrounded by a light border of green.

'Beedham's White', bright yellow leaves and white flowers.

'Chequers', somewhat more vigorous, flowers pinkish, leaves larger than the species.

'Orchid Frost', selected by Mike Bovio for abundant orchid pink flowers, bright silver foliage edged in green.

'Pink Pewter', pink flowers atop coarsely toothed dark silver, green-edged foliage.

'Purple Dragon', many deep purple flowers, silver foliage trimmed in green. Very popular

'Shell Pink', soft pink flowers, leaves with irregular white variegation in their centers.

'White Nancy', leaves similar to 'Beacon Silver', flowers white.

Lamium maculatum 'Beacon Silver'

Lamium maculatum 'Beedham's White'

Lamium maculatum
'Pink Pewter'

Lamium maculatum
'Purple Dragon'

Lamium maculatum
'Shell Pink'

Lampranthus spectabilis
(photo by Richard Shiell)

Lantana ×*hybrida*

Lavandula angustifolia
'Baby Blue'

Lampranthus spectabilis
Showy ice plant, trailing ice plant

Outstanding for its bright colorful flowers and glistening water-soaked leaves and stems, showy ice plant is resistant to fire and is therefore a good choice for rest areas and along sidewalks and foundations of public buildings. It works well as a soil stabilizer on highway embankments and gently sloping berms. It makes a splendid specimen in rock gardens and in elevated planters, terrace plantings, alongside stairways, and atop retaining walls. Zones 9–11. South Africa.

A succulent 15 in. (38 cm) tall by 18–24 in. (45–60 cm) wide. Leaves 2–3 in. (5.0–7.5 cm) long by ¼ in. (6 mm) wide, gray with reddish tips. Flowers numerous, bright purple, 2–3 in. (5.0–7.5 cm) wide.

Moderate growing; space 10–18 in. (25–45 cm) apart. Any well-drained soil. Very drought tolerant. Full sun.

Lantana ×hybrida
Hybrid lantana

The cultivated hybrid lantanas are sturdy, woody based covers for warm climates in moderate to large areas, on flat and sloping terrain, and particularly in elevated beds or planters. They bear bright, cheerful, fragrant flowers and are useful in controlling erosion, as accent plants in borders, or as edging along paths and walkways. Zones 9–11.

A low-growing, spreading or trailing perennial 2–3 ft. (60–90 cm) high, 4–8 ft. (1.2–2.4 m) across. Leaves coarse, evergreen or deciduous, edged with teeth, smell somewhat like citrus when touched. Flowers brightly colored, in hemispherical heads, changing color as they mature, pleasant smelling, spring, sparsely in other seasons. Fruit a poisonous, berrylike drupe, green turning to blackish.

Fast growing; space 3–4 ft. (90–120 cm) apart. Any soil with good drainage. Drought tolerant, but needs an occasional deep watering in summer. Shear annually to stimulate new growth.

'American Red', bright red and yellow flowers.

'Athens Rose', rose-colored flowers aging to pink.

'Carnival', flowers mixed pink, yellow, lavender, and crimson.

'Christine', bright cerise-pink flowers.

'Confetti', flowers yellow, pink, or purple.

'Cream Carpet', flowers creamy white with bright yellow throats.

'Gold Rush', masses of golden yellow flowers.

'Irene', compact habit, flowers lemon-yellow and magenta.

'Kathleen', flowers rose-pink with golden centers.

'Miss Huff', orange and pink flowers.

'Snow White', deep shiny green foliage, snow white flowers with a yellow center.

'Sunburst', flowers bright yellow.

'Variegata', leaves green with chartreuse edges and mottling, flowers lemon-yellow.

Lavandula angustifolia
True lavender

Among the most popular garden plants, true lavender is sometimes used as a specimen in an herb garden but often overlooked as a ground cover. It is valuable for edging walkways and garden borders and can also be used as a foundation plant or rock garden specimen. Zones 5–9. Southern Europe, North Africa.

A semiwoody subshrub 18–30 in. (45–75 cm) tall, spreading 12–24 in. (30–60 cm) across. Leaves evergreen, narrowly oblong, pleasantly aromatic, 2 in. (5 cm) long by ¼ in. (6 mm) wide, blue-green. Flowers small, pinkish purple, in spikes, mid to late summer.

Moderate growing; space 14–18 in. (35–45 cm) apart. Well-drained, light-textured, slightly acidic to slightly alkaline loam. Very drought tolerant, but benefits from occasional deep watering during summer. Full sun. Trim after flowering to keep plantings neat and to insure abundant flowers the next year.

'Baby Blue', compact habit, many deep blue flowers.

'Baby White', 12 in. (30 cm) tall, pure white flowers.

'Beccles Pink', compact habit, many pink flowers.

Lavandula angustifolia 'Hidcote Pink"

Lavandula angustifolia 'Lady Lavender'

'Bowles' Early', very fragrant lavender flowers.

'Hidcote', 15–20 in. (35–45 cm) tall, rich purple-blue flowers.

'Hidcote Pink', pink flowers.

'Lady Lavender', frosty green leaves, open habit, intensely purple flowers.

'Munstead', 18 in. (40 cm) tall, dark lavender-blue flowers.

'Nana', 12 in. (30 cm) tall, purple flowers.

'Rosea', rose-pink flowers.

'Royal Velvet', fragrant dark purple flowers.

'Sachet', superior fragrance, violet flowers.

'Silver Edge', foliage variegated creamy white and silvery blue, flowers violet-blue.

'Silver Frost', powdery white frosted foliage, bluish lavender flowers.

Leptinella linearifolia

LEPTINELLA

The approximately 30 *Leptinella* species, formerly assigned to the genus *Cotula*, are good filler plants for cracks and crevices. Zones 5–10. Southern Hemisphere.

Fast growing; space 8–12 in. (20–30 cm) apart. Slightly moistened, well-drained, rich, acidic loam. Full sun to light shade. Trim back shoots as they outgrow their bounds.

Leptinella linearifolia
A tufted perennial. Unlike all the other *Leptinella* species, which have compound leaves, this species has entire leaves.

Leptinella minor
Miniature brass buttons
A rhizomatous herb ½ in. (12 mm) tall. Leaves medium green. Flowers tiny, yellow, ball shaped, summer.

Leptinella minor

Leptinella squalida
New Zealand brass buttons
Sometimes used as a turf substitute on a small scale. A diminutive, mat-forming herb 2–4 in. (5–10 cm) tall, spreading 2 ft. (60 cm) across. Leaves evergreen, fernlike, soft-textured, hairy, narrowly oval, bronzy green, 2 in. (5 cm) long. Flowers buttonlike, yellow, relatively nonshowy, above the foliage, summer.

Leptinella squalida

Leptinella squalida 'Platt's Black'

Leucothoe fontanesiana 'Gerard's Rainbow'

Ligularia dentata 'Dark Beauty'

'Platt's Black', 1/2–1 in. (12–25 mm) tall with blackish purple foliage often tipped in green.

Leucothoe fontanesiana
Dog hobble, switch ivy

With its gracefully arching, fountainlike branch pattern, dog hobble makes an excellent general cover and facing plant for moderate to large areas. It is useful for binding soil on sloping terrain. When in bloom, the shiny, dark green branches make lovely cut flowers. Zones 4–6. Virginia to Georgia and Tennessee.

A rhizomatous subshrub 2–4 ft. (60–120 cm) tall, spreading somewhat less than twice that in width. Leaves evergreen, simple, leathery, dark shiny green, elliptic to narrowly oblong, tapering to an abrupt point, 2–5 1/4 in. (5–13 cm) long by 1–1 1/2 in. (2.5–4.0 cm) wide. Flowers small, downward-hanging, urn shaped, white, fragrant, spring.

Slow to moderate growing; space 30–42 in. (75–105 cm) apart. Well-drained, rich, acidic loam. Very drought tolerant. Protect from strong, drying winds. Light to dense shade.

'Girard's Rainbow' (syn. 'Rainbow'), new growth green, later developing yellowish, pinkish, and whitish splotches.

'Nana', compact habit reaching 2 ft. (60 cm) tall by 6 ft. (1.8 m) wide.

Ligularia dentata
Bigleaf ligularia

A rugged, coarse-textured herb 3–4 ft. (90–120 cm) tall. Leaves very attractive, deep green, kidney shaped, to 20 in. (50 cm) wide, margins coarsely toothed, Flowers orange, daisylike, above the foliage, mid to late summer. Zones 5–8. China.

Moist soil. Cool shade.

Although the species isn't particularly common, it has given rise to several outstanding selections.

'Britt-Marie Crawford', exceptional, leaves deep dark chocolaty above and dark purple below, flowers golden orange and daisylike atop purplish black stems.

'Dark Beauty', fabulous coarsely textured leaves purplish green above and intensely maroon-purple below.

'Desdemona', new foliage beet-red changing to greenish bronze with purplish undersides, flowers golden yellow.

'Othello', like 'Desdemona', but somewhat taller.

'Sommergold', green leaves and deep orange flowers.

Ligularia tussilaginea
Daempfer golden-ray

Flaunting some of the most magnificent foliage of any ground cover, this sizable herb (now called *Farfugium japonicum* by some taxonomists) makes a bold statement and, considering its preference for shady terrain, is no less impressive for its show of golden yellow flowers. Often it is used as a walkway or border edging and as a facing to trees. It is best on a moderate to large scale, but a single clump (especially of the colorful cultivars) stands out as a unique specimen. Zones 6–10. Japan, China, Korea, Taiwan.

A creeping perennial 18–24 in. (45–60 cm) tall, spreading indefinitely. Leaves evergreen, gigantic, kidney shaped, medium to dark green, 6 in. (15 cm) long by 12 in. (30 cm) wide, edged with shallow teeth, covered with fine hairs when young, becoming shiny and hairless as they mature. Flowers daisylike, yellow, 1½–2½ in. (4–6 cm) in diameter, mid summer.

Moderate growing; space 18–24 in. (45–60 cm) apart. Constantly moist, rich, slightly acidic loam. Moderate to dense shade in warm climates and inland, more sun or morning sun with afternoon shade in cool climates and coastal areas where soil remains slightly moist in summer.

'Argentea', leaves irregularly mottled dark green, gray-green, and ivory.

'Aurea-maculata', leopard plant, dark green leaves randomly dappled with bright round yellow spots.

'Crispata', parsley ligularia, leaf edges ruffled and crinkled.

Ligularia tussilaginea 'Aurea-maculata'

Ligularia tussilaginea 'Gigantea'

'Gigantea', shiny deep green, nearly round foliage, flowers yellow.

'Kin Kan', 15 in. (38 cm) tall, shiny green leaves edged in creamy white, flowers yellow.

LIRIOPE
Lily-turf

Exceptional for edging borders or lining walks and driveways, lily-turf is often used as a facer of trees and foundations, and as a turf substitute in moderate to large areas. Small groups of plants can be used for accent, and single specimens of the nonrunning forms can add a striking vertical dimension in shaded corners of the rock garden. Lily-turfs are widely used in Asian garden settings. See also *Ophiopogon*.

Liriope muscari 'Royal Purple'

Liriope spicata 'Silver Dragon'

Liriope muscari
Blue lily-turf

A clumplike, tuberous-rooted (potato-like), grassy, lilylike species 18–24 in. (45–60 cm) high, spreading 8–12 in. (20–30 cm) wide. Leaves narrow, evergreen, 2 ft. (60 cm) long by 3/4 in. (2 cm) wide, dark green. Flowers dark purple, 1/4 in. (6 mm) wide, in spikelike clusters above the foliage, partially hidden in mature plants, mid to late summer. Fruit showy, round, green, ripening to shiny black. Zones 6–10, a few cultivars to Zone 5. Japan, China.

Slow growing; space 12–16 in. (30–40 cm) apart.

'Big Blue', deep blue flowers, erect leaves, Zone 5.

'Christmas Tree', light purple flowers in clusters tapering to a point like a Christmas tree.

'Evergreen Giant', taller with stiffly upright habit.

'Gold Band', leaves shorter, broader, and edged in gold.

'John Burch', very large leaved with cockscomb-shaped flower clusters.

'Lilac Beauty', shorter, with deep violet flowers.

'Majestic', many deep violet flowers.

'Monroe's White', pure white flowers.

'Okina', new foliage snow white, gradually turning mint green over time, lilac-purple flowers.

'Peedee Ingot', golden yellow leaves in full sun, chartreuse leaves in shade, lavender-blue flowers.

'Royal Purple', dark purple flowers.

'Silver Midget', low growing to 8 in. (20 cm), foliage narrowly banded with white.

'Silvery Sunproof', leaves pale green with white to yellow stripes, tolerates more sun, blooms profusely, Zone 5.

'Variegata', new leaves with yellow edges that become green their second year, 12–18 in. (30–45 cm) tall, with violet flowers.

'Webster's Wideleaf', very broad leaves, tuft-forming.

Any well-drained neutral to acidic soil. Drought tolerant. Full sun to moderately dense shade. Mow in spring, before new growth begins, to promote a healthy, youthful appearance and to stimulate vigor.

Liriope muscari 'Variegata'

Liriope spicata

Liriope spicata
Creeping lily-turf
A rhizomatous lilylike herb 8–12 in. (20–30 cm) tall, spreading 6–12 in. (15–30 cm) wide. Leaves evergreen, straplike, to 18 in. (45 cm) long by ¼ in. (6 mm) wide, dark green, turning bronzy green in late winter. Flowers ¾ in. (6 mm) wide, pale violet to white, in spikelike clusters on purple stems, mid to late summer. Fruit a blue-black berrylike round capsule. Zones 4–10. Japan, China.

Lithodora diffusa 'Grace Ward'

Moderate growing; space 8–16 in. (20–40 cm) apart.

'Silver Dragon', dark green leaves with silvery white longitudinal variegation, producing shoots of all-green leaves.

Lithodora diffusa
Spreading lithodora

Spreading lithodora performs well as a small-scale general cover. As a specimen or accent plant in rock gardens and border settings it combines effectively with acid-loving shrubs. Zones 6–8. Southern and western Europe, Morocco.

A horizontally growing shrublet 6–12 in. (15–30 cm) tall, spreading 24–30 in. (60–75 cm) across. Leaves hairy, evergreen, dark green above, grayish below, $\frac{1}{2}$ in. (12 mm) long by $\frac{1}{8}$–$\frac{1}{4}$ in. (3–6 mm) wide. Flowers funnel shaped, $\frac{1}{2}$ in. (12 mm) wide, iridescent blue, spring and early summer.

Moderate growing; space 18–30 in. (45–75 cm) apart. Moist, fertile, well-drained acidic soil. Light to moderate shade.

Lonicera japonica 'Aureo-reticulata'

Lonicera japonica 'Halliana'

'Alba', white flowers.
'Grace Ward', dark blue flowers.
'Heavenly Blue', sky blue flowers.
'Lohbrunner White', white flowers.

LONICERA
Honeysuckle

Ground-covering honeysuckles share many of the same traits (beautiful fragrant flowers, shiny deciduous or evergreen foliage) as the more common shrubby and climbing forms that have so popularized the genus. They excel in moderate to large open areas, particularly in elevated planters around building foundations or as soil stabilizers on large, open slopes.

Most acidic to alkaline soils with good drainage. Very to moderately drought tolerant; requires only an infrequent deep watering in hot, dry weather. Full sun to light shade. Prune heavily in late winter. Use an elevated lawn mower to remove dead undergrowth. Later in the season cut back leading stems as they outgrow their bounds or begin to climb trees or shrubs.

Lonicera japonica
Japanese honeysuckle

Because it grabs hold of and strangles other plants, it should be planted by itself or with trees whose trunks are too broad for it to grip. Its use is outlawed in some states due to invasiveness, particularly where the growing season is long enough for plants to set seed that may be moved long distances by birds. Use it only in cooler climates where it has proven to not set seed.

A climbing vine 8–16 in. (20–40 cm) tall when supported, spreading indefinitely. Leaves semievergreen to evergreen, oval to oval-oblong, 1¼–3 in. (3.0–7.5 cm) long, shiny green, often becoming yellowish during autumn. Flowers white with pink or purplish tinges, maturing to yellow, 1½ in. (4 cm) long, fragrant, early summer. Fruit black, berrylike, ¼ in. (6 mm) wide, ripening early to mid autumn. Zones 5–9. Japan.

Moderate to fast growing; space 12–30 in. (30–75 cm) apart.

'Aureo-reticulata', yellow-net honeysuckle, leaves to 2 in. (5 cm) long, colored bright green

Lonicera japonica 'Hall's Prolific'

with striking yellow or golden veins, best in shade and rich, moist soil.

'Halliana', pure white flowers age to yellow.

'Hall's Prolific', like 'Halliana' but bearing many more flowers.

'Purpurea', a bit less vigorous, leaves bluish purple below and greenish purple above, flowers purplish red with white interiors.

Lonicera pileata
Royal carpet honeysuckle

A neat, low-spreading, shrubby habit 12–18 in. (30–45 cm) tall, 3–4 ft. (90–120 cm) wide. Leaves semievergreen, oval to narrowly oblong, ½–1¼ in. (12–30 mm) long, less than ½ in. (12 mm) wide, medium green. Flowers fragrant, yellowish white, about ¼ in. (6 mm) long, not showy, often almost unnoticed during mid spring. Fruit berrylike, small, violet-purple, translucent. Zones 7–9. China.

Lotus corniculatus
Bird's-foot trefoil

Bird's-foot trefoil is often used to prevent erosion on a small to large scale, particularly in infertile sandy soil. Like other members of the pea family, it can convert soilborne atmospheric nitrogen into a form the plant can use. Zones 5–10. Europe, Asia.

A matlike, trailing, semiwoody herb 1½–2 in. (4–5 cm) tall, spreading 2 ft. (60 cm) across. Leaves composed of three narrowly oval leaflets, medium to dark green. Flowers yellow with red tinges, in clusters, pealike, ½–¾ in. (12–20 mm) long, summer. Fruit a slender green pod 1 in. (2.5 cm) long.

Moderate to fast growing; space 14–24 in. (35–60 cm) apart. Somewhat infertile, gritty or sandy, well-drained alkaline soils. Marginally drought tolerant; needs supplemental water in extended periods of heat and drought. Full sun.

Lonicera pileata

Lotus corniculatus

Lotus corniculatus
'Pleniflorus'

Lysimachia clethroides

Lysimachia nummularia 'Aurea'

Lysimachia ciliata 'Purpurea'

'Pleniflorus', double flowers, not as likely to become weedy as it does not set seed. Recommended over the species, which in some climates may become invasive.

LYSIMACHIA
Loosestrife
The loosestrifes mentioned here spread readily and therefore should be planted only where they can be contained.

Most soil conditions, possibly with the exception of gravelly soils. Best in constant soil moisture; tolerant of boggy conditions. Light to moderate shade. Trim back or dig up the trailing stems as they outgrow their bounds.

Lysimachia ciliata 'Purpurea'
Purple fringed loosestrife
A perennial herb 2–4 in. (5–10 cm) tall. Leaves purple, fringed. Flowers yellow. Zones 3–10.

Lysimachia clethroides
Gooseneck loosestrife
Used on a moderate to large scale as general cover or contained as an accent or companion plant. A tenacious, rhizomatous herb 2–3 ft. (60–90 cm) tall. Leaves deciduous, oval to lance shaped, medium green, tapered at both ends, 3–6 in. (7.5–15.0 cm) long by ³⁄₄ to 1¹⁄₄ in. (2–3 cm) wide. Flowers numerous, white, on arching, gooseneck shaped racemes, summer, attractive to butterflies. Zones 3–9. China, Japan.

Fast growing; space 18–24 in. (45–60 cm) apart.

'Geisha', green foliage broadly and irregularly edged in yellowish gold.

Lysimachia nummularia
Creeping Charley, creeping Jenny
Because this creeper can smother short, less-assertive neighbors, it should not be combined with other low-growing plants. Neither should it be sited along the periphery of one's property—out of respect for neighbors and to prevent it from creeping into natural areas. It makes a mossy blanket in contained areas underneath low-growing trees and shrubs. Used in elevated planters where its stems can trail over like a waterfall, creeping Charley is at its best. It performs admirably as a turf substitute in smaller contained areas or along the edge of a stream or pond, and it is ideal between stepping stones and alongside wooded garden paths.

A tenacious herb 1–2 in. (2.5–5.0 cm) tall, spreading indefinitely. Leaves evergreen, nearly round, to 1 in. (2.5 cm) wide, medium to dark green. Flowers buttercup yellow, ³⁄₄ in. (2 cm) wide, early summer. Zones 4–9. Europe, central Russia; naturalized in North America.

Moderate to fast growing; space 10–16 in. (25–40 cm) apart.

'Aurea', golden creeping Charley, exceptionally bright golden leaves, slower growing but also pretty fast by most standards.

Mahonia nervosa
Cascades mahonia, Oregon grape
Cascades mahonia is excellent as a specimen in rock gardens, as edging alongside walkways, and as a facing to shrubby border plantings. Between its flowers, fruit, and foliage, it is interesting year-round. Zones 6–9. British Columbia to California.

A low, rhizomatous, woody shrub 12–18 in. (30–45 cm) tall, spreading 4–5 ft. (1.2–1.5 m) wide. Leaves evergreen, 7–16 in. (18–40 cm) long, composed of 11 to 19 dark green spiny

Mahonia nervosa

Mazus reptans

Melissa officinalis

Mentha requienii

toothed leaflets, each 2–3 in. (5.0–7.5 cm) long, reddish in winter. Flowers yellow, in clusters to 8 in. (20 cm) wide, late summer. Fruit a round, blue-black berry.

Slow growing; space 12–16 in. (30–40 cm) apart. Slightly moist but well-drained, rich, mildly acidic soil. Moderately drought tolerant. Full sun to light shade; afternoon shade in areas of hot, dry summers. Protect from wind and sun in winter. Lightly prune in late summer to promote compactness.

Mazus reptans
Creeping mazus

A single plant holds the potential for a quick, efficient cover or for weediness, depending upon your interpretation. It bears curious purple flowers, cheerful green foliage, and is best in small areas, particularly as a carpet underneath small trees and tall single-stemmed shrubs. It also is an effective filler between stepping stones and an edger around a shaded patio. Finally, it is rather interesting lining the banks of a shaded reflecting pool or koi pond. Zones 4–9. Himalayas.

A low-growing, rooting herb that spreads indefinitely. Leaves semievergreen, light green, almost succulent, to 2 in. (5 cm) long, somewhat oval, more or less toothed about the edges. Flowers reach 3/4 in. (2 cm) long, composed of two halves (lips), violet-blue, uppermost lip composed of two lobes, lowermost lip composed of three lobes, each white with yellow and purple spots, late spring.

Slow growing initially, then moderate to fast growing; space 8–12 in. (20–30 cm) apart. Well-drained, rich loam. Frequent watering during the summer, particularly if grown in sandy soils. Full sun to moderate shade.

Melissa officinalis
Lemon balm, bee balm

Frequently included in herb or scent gardens for its leaves that give off a very sweet lemony aroma each time they are brushed against, this herb should not be overlooked as a ground cover. It works well as a backdrop to lower-growing herbs and ground covers whose leaf color contrasts with its own. It is also an ideal edging to walkway and garden paths. Zone 5. Southern Europe, western and central Asia.

A dense, erect or sprawling herb 14–24 in. (35–60 cm) tall, to more than 2 ft. (60 cm) across. Leaves vibrant medium green, deciduous, simple, oval to heart shaped, 1–3 in. (2.5–7.5 cm) long by 2 in. (5 cm) wide, edged with rounded teeth, covered with furrows and sparse hairs. Flowers small, white, somewhat-trumpet shaped, above the leaf mass, summer.

Moderate growing; space 8–12 in. (20–30 cm) apart. Slightly moistened but well-drained, rich, slightly acidic loam. Full sun.

'**All Gold**', golden leaves turning to green in summer.

'**Aurea**', yellow leaves later turning green.

'**Lime**', leaves lime scented.

'**Variegata**', variegated yellow and green leaves later turning all green.

Mentha requienii
Corsican mint, creeping mint

The original source of flavoring for the drink crème de menthe, Corsican mint is excellent for filling the cracks between stepping stones and patio blocks and as a small-scale lawn substitute. Zones 6–10. Corsica.

A matlike herb 1/2–1 1/2 in. (12–40 mm) tall. Leaves tidy, oval to round or heart shaped, 1/8–3/16 in. (3–5 mm) long, dark green, strongly aromatic. Flowers tiny, lavender, summer.

Slow growing; space 6–19 in. (15–48 cm) apart. Any slightly moistened to saturated soil. Full sun to light shade.

Microbiota decussata
Siberian cypress

This evergreen conifer resembles a feathery leaved, horizontal juniper. It attractively displays its foliage upon gracefully drooping branches and imparts a lush tranquilizing effect to the landscape. Mass plantings may be used to face foundations, and single plants may be used as specimens on sloping terrain where their beauty can be more fully appreciated. Zones 2–8. Siberia.

Microbiota decussata

A low-growing, woody shrub 8 in. (20 cm) tall, spreading 9–12 ft. (60 cm) across. Leaves fragrant, scalelike or awl shaped, soft and leathery, dull green, turning bronzy almost burgundy in autumn, persisting through winter.

Moderate growing; space 3½–5 ft. (105–150 cm) apart. Any well-drained soil. Moderately drought tolerant, but welcomes an occasional deep watering in summer. Full sun to light shade.

Mitchella repens
Partridge berry, twinberry

Attractive for its evergreen foliage, dainty flowers, and bright red fruit, partridge berry is used on a small to moderate scale and is particularly well adapted for shady naturalized settings. Zones 5–9. Eastern North America.

A semiwoody, trailing, vinelike species 1 in. (2.5 cm) tall, spreading indefinitely. Leaves round to oval, ¾ in. (2 cm) long, glossy dark green with whitish veins. Flowers pinkish, funnel shaped, to ½ in. (12 mm) long, early summer. Fruit an eight-seeded, brilliant scarlet berry, ¼ in. (6 mm) in diameter, ripening in fall, persisting through winter.

Slow growing; space 6–8 in. (15–20 cm) apart. Moist, rich, acidic loam.

Var. *leucocarpa*, pale yellowish white fruit.

Muehlenbeckia axillaris
Creeping wire vine

A valuable ground cover for moderate to large contained areas, creeping wire vine can be used as a foot-friendly filler to stepping stones or on sloping terrain where it controls erosion. Its high salt tolerance makes it useful in seaside landscapes. Zones 5–10. Australia, New Zealand, Tasmania.

A relatively small, sprawling, mounding, semiwoody, matlike vine 2–4 in. (5–10 cm) tall, spreading 4–5 ft. (1.2–1.5 m) wide. Leaves evergreen, ⅜ in. (9 mm) long, oblong to round, dark green to bronzy green with reddish edges. Flowers yellowish green, insignificant. Fruit a shiny black nutlike seed surrounded by a shiny white, berrylike covering.

Mitchella repens

Mitchella repens, fruit

Muehlenbeckia axillaris (photo by Pamela Harper)

Myoporum parvifolium

Slow to moderate growing; space 12–15 in. (30–40 cm) apart. Light-textured, well-drained, slightly acidic to slightly alkaline soils. Tolerant of short periods of drought, but prefers moderately moist soil at all times. Full sun to light shade. Trim back the trailing stems as they outgrow their bounds.

Myoporum parvifolium

This shrub is a staple for many warm coastal and arid climates, where its lush green appearance, few maintenance needs, and drought tolerance make it one of the best ground covers. It is usually planted on a moderate to large scale as a general cover and foundation facer. The fleshy leaves and stems store moisture, making it a good choice for public locations, where people are apt to discard cigarettes or matches. Because myoporum roots well and forms dense mats, it is excellent on slopes and along highway embankments for erosion control. Zones 9–11. New Zealand.

A woody, low-growing, horizontally spreading shrub 3–6 in. (7.5–15.0 cm) tall, 9 ft. (2.7 m) across. Leaves evergreen, more or less lance shaped, to ½ in. (12 mm) long by ¼ in. (6 mm) wide, edged at the tip with irregular teeth, bright green, with purplish tints in winter. Flowers waxy, white, starlike, ⅜ in. (9 mm) across, spring and summer. Fruit a tiny purplish berry ⅛ in. (3 mm) in diameter.

Moderate to fast growing; space 3–5 ft. (90–150 cm) apart. Well-drained, slightly acidic sandy loam. Drought tolerant. Full sun. Trim back growth periodically when stems outgrow their bounds. Mow occasionally to rejuvenate growth and to keep plantings neat.

'Burgundy Carpet', 6 in. (15 cm) tall by 6–8 ft. (1.8–2.4 m) wide, tips of new stems and leaves deep reddish purple when grown in sun.

'Fine Leaf Form', 6–12 in. (15–30 cm) tall, narrower foliage.

'Pink', clear pink flowers.

'Putah Creek', more symmetrical in habit, 12 in. (30 cm) tall by more than 4 ft. (1.2 m) wide.

Myosotis scorpioides
True forget-me-not

True forget-me-not (aka swamp forget-me-not) is used as a long-blooming general cover for small to moderate areas, where its soft, lacy, delicate texture softens up hard lines of brick or wood structures and coarse-textured trees and shrubs. It works well near streams, ponds, and lakes, and is useful in boggy areas and at poolside. Zones 5–9. Europe to Siberia.

A rhizomatous herb. Leaves simple, oblong to lance shaped, bright shiny green, deciduous, 2 in. (5 cm) long. Flowers small, bright blue to pink (sometimes with a yellow, pink, or white eye), spring and summer.

Myosotis scorpioides

Moderate growing; space 8–12 in. (20–30 cm) apart. Neutral to acidic, moist to wet soils. Protect from wind. Sun to moderate shade. Divide plants every fourth or fifth year to improve bloom.

'Alba', white flowers.

'Pinkie', 12 in. (30 cm) tall, clear pink flowers.

'Rosea', pink flowers.

'Sapphire', brilliant sapphire blue flowers.

'Semperflorens', dwarf habit, many flowers.

Nandina domestica
Heavenly bamboo, sacred bamboo

A woody based, semievergreen, multistemmed suckering shrub, heavenly bamboo reaches 6–8 ft. (1.8–2.4 m) tall and wide, but its dwarf selections are useful as ground covers. They can be planted as a low hedging along walkways, arranged in small groups near the trunk of a tree or next to a garden ornament or large boulder to create accent, or massed in moderate to large groups and used for erosion control or foundation facing. They are particularly effective if the background is light colored. They combine well with ornamental grasses and sprawling ground covers. The fruit provides wintertime food for songbirds. Zones 7–9. Central China, Japan.

Leaves composed of two or three elliptic leaflets, each one 1–3½ in. (2.5–9.0 cm) long by 1–1½ in. (2.5–4.0 mm) wide, leathery, young leaves often tinged pink or bronzy as they open, becoming light green in summer, picking up bronzy or purplish hues in fall. Flowers small, pinkish in bud, in erect panicles 8–15 in. (20–38 cm) long. Fruit a small bright red berry.

Slow to moderate growing; space 2–3 ft. (60–90 cm) apart. Fertile, acidic loam. Drought tolerant; needs occasional deep watering in summer. Full sun. Remove the oldest stems annually just above the crown.

Nandina domestica 'Atropurpurea Nana'

'Atropurpurea Nana' (syn. 'Purpurea Dwarf'), stiff upright habit, to 2 ft. (60 cm) tall, reddish purple leaves in fall.

'Firepower', to 30 in. (75 cm) tall and wide, brilliant crimson fall and winter foliage.

'Gulf Stream', 30–42 in. (75–105 cm) tall, compact habit, metallic blue-green foliage that turns intensely red in fall.

'Harbor Dwarf', a graceful mound, 2–3 ft. (60–90 cm) tall, leaves orange to bronzy red or purple-tinged in fall.

'Lemon Hill', only 12 in. (30 cm) tall, lemon yellow fruit.

'Moon Bay', 3 ft. (90 cm) tall, compact habit, bright lime green fine-textured foliage that turns scarlet in fall.

'Nana' (syn. 'Compacta'), 2–4 ft. (60–120 cm) tall, dense mounds, fruiting less than the species.

'Pygmaea' (syn. 'Minima'), 3 ft. (90 cm) tall, leaves bright red in fall.

'Wood's Dwarf', compact habit, leaves crimson-orange in fall.

Nepeta ×faassenii
Faassen's catmint, mauve catmint

This attractive, long-blooming natural hybrid is valuable as a small- to large-scale general cover, erosion controller, foundation facer, accent plant, pathway edger, or rock garden specimen. Like catnip (*Nepeta cataria*), it attracts cats, and its flowers furnish nectar for hummingbirds. Zones 4–9. Of garden origin.

A mound-forming herb 18–24 in. (45–60 cm) tall, spreading 2–3 ft. (60–90 cm) across. Leaves deciduous to semievergreen, oblong to oval, 1¼ in. (3 cm) long, edged with rounded teeth, gray-green, aromatic when crushed. Flowers violet-blue, above the leaves, summer.

Moderate growing; space 12–18 in. (30–45 cm) apart. Any well-drained soil. Good drought tolerance. Full sun. Shear mid summer for repeat

Nepeta ×faassenii 'Blue Wonder'

Nepeta ×*faassenii* 'Six Hills Giant'

Nierembergia hippomanica var. *violacea*

blooming and to keep plants compact, rejuvenated, and neat looking.

'Blue Ice', 12–15 in. (30–38 cm) tall, white flowers with blue tint.

'Blue Wonder', 12–15 in. (30–38 cm) tall, dark blue flowers.

'Dropmore', deep lavender flowers.

'Kit Kat', 10 in. (22 cm) tall, dark purple-blue flowers.

'Six Hills Giant' (sometimes classified as *Nepeta gigantea*), very imposing, foliage 3 ft. (90 cm) tall by 4 ft. (1.2 m) wide, flowers dark violet.

'Snowflake', white flowers.

'Walker's Low', 15–18 in. (38– 45 cm) tall, mound forming, many lavender-blue flowers.

'White Wonder', 12–15 in. (30–38 cm) tall, white flowers.

Nierembergia hippomanica var. *violacea*
Dwarf cupflower

Dwarf cupflower performs well as a small-scale general cover and combines beautifully with thyme, candytuft (*Iberis*), and *Cymbalaria* species, especially in rock gardens. Zones 7–10. South America.

A sprawling herb 6–12 in. (15–30 cm) tall. Leaves bright green, oblong to spatula shaped, 1¼ in. (3 cm) long. Flowers bell shaped, blue to violet, 1 in. (2.5 cm) wide, summer.

Moderate growing; space 12 in. (30 cm) part. Slightly moistened, fertile, well-drained soil. Full sun in cool climates; light shade in warm climates. Mow or trim back plants during early spring before new growth occurs.

'Purple Robe', darker violet flowers.

Oenothera berlandieri
Mexican primrose

Attractive for its foliage and exceptional floral display, Mexican primrose works well as a general cover for facing taller shrubs (especially dark green evergreens), garden ornaments, and foundations. It is recommended for locations of high visibility, where passersby can appreciate its beauty, such as on slopes, in parking strips, or as edging for walkways or borders. Zones 5–9. Texas, Mexico.

A low-growing herb 6–12 in. (15–30 cm) tall. Leaves evergreen, narrowly oblong to oval, 1–3 in. (2.5–7.5 cm) long, gray-green. Flowers rose-pink, day-blooming, spring.

Moderate to fast growing; space 14–18 in. (35–45 cm) apart. Well-drained, rich, sandy to loamy, acidic to slightly alkaline soils. Tolerant of heat and drought. Full sun to light shade. Mow in early spring.

'Siskiyou', 10 in. (25 cm) tall, with large silvery pink flowers.

Oenothera berlandieri 'Siskiyou'

Ophiopogon japonicus, as a filler between stepping stones

Ophiopogon japonicus, as a ground cover

OPHIOPOGON
Dwarf lily-turf

Like *Liriope*, the genus *Ophiopogon* displays grassy foliage, dainty yet showy flowers, and shiny dark fruit. The evergreen leaves are smaller and more refined than those of *Liriope* and they arch over to form a graceful fountain shape. The flowers are white or lilac, and the fruit blue. *Ophiopogon* can be used in the same manner as *Liriope* but on a somewhat smaller scale.

Most slightly moist but well-drained soils. Full sun in coastal areas; light to moderate shade further inland.

Ophiopogon japonicus
Mondo grass

A dense sod-forming, no-mow turf substitute 6–15 in. (15–38 cm) tall, spreading indefinitely. Leaves evergreen, grasslike, 10–15 in. (25–38 cm) long, dark green. Flowers light lilac to white, ¼ in. (6 mm) wide, early summer. Fruit a blue

Ophiopogon planiscapus 'Nigrescens'

globe-shaped capsule to ¼ in. (6 mm) wide. Zones 7–9. Japan, Korea.

Slow to moderate growing; space 10–14 in. (25–35 cm) apart.

'Comet', leaves with narrow vertical white stripes.

Var. *compacta*, only 2 in. (5 cm) tall and 6 in. (15 cm) wide.

'Nippon', only 2 in. (5 cm) tall by 3–4 in. (7.5–10.0 cm) wide.

'Silver Mist', leaves longitudinally variegated white and green, relatively slow growing.

'Silver Showers', leaves striped white.

'Super Dwarf', only 1 in. (2.5 cm) tall.

Ophiopogon planiscapus
'Nigrescens'
Black lily-turf

Known for its unusual foliage, which provides outstanding contrast when combined with lighter-foliaged plants. A unique selection 6–12 in. (15–30 cm) tall, spreading indefinitely. Leaves evergreen, grasslike, 12 in. (30 cm) long by ¼ in. (6 mm) wide, appearing black. Flowers bell shaped, pinkish to purplish, ¼ in. (6 mm) long, summer. Fruit a blackish berry. Zones 5–10. Japan.

Slow growing; space 4 in. (10 cm) apart.

Origanum laevigatum
Ornamental oregano

Typically used along sidewalks, on sloping terrain, and in planters, ornamental oregano provides both foliar and floral interest and is complementary to a host of clump-forming or shy-spreading species. Zones 5–9. Asia Minor and Syria in rocky mountainous sites.

Leaves dark gray-green, ⅜–½ in. (9–12 mm) long, triangular-oval. Flowers numerous, purple, butterfly-attracting, summer to early fall.

Moderate growing; space 10–12 in. (25–30 cm) apart. Gritty or gravelly, well-drained but moisture-retentive soil. Drought tolerant. Full sun. Give plants a hard pruning in early spring to rejuvenate and promote compactness.

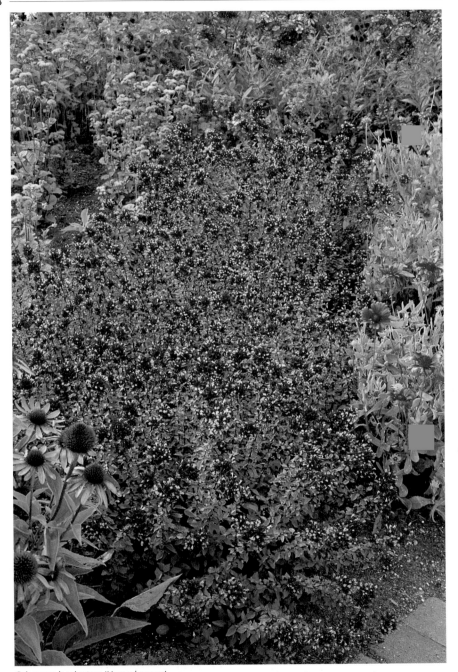

Origanum laevigatum 'Herrenhausen'

Origanum laevigatum 'Rosenkuppel'

'Herrenhausen', 15 in. (38 cm) tall, young leaves suffused with burgundy, lavender flowers with deep red-violet bracts.

'Hopley's Purple', 12–20 in. (30–50 cm) tall, sprays of tiny purple flowers resembling baby's breath.

'Pilgrim', 12–16 in. (30–40 cm) tall, blue-green foliage, tiny pink flowers surrounded by purple bracts during summer.

'Rosenkuppel', like 'Herrenhausen', but with vibrant pinkish flowers that begin about two weeks earlier.

Osteospermum fruticosum
Trailing African daisy, freeway daisy

Known to many Californians as freeway daisy, this excellent general cover or soil stabilizer for slopes, berms, terraces, and highway embankments is usually used in moderate to large plantings. High salt tolerance allows it to be used near the shore as well as inland. It is also considered to be relatively fire retardant. Zones 9–11. South Africa.

A low-growing, thick, mat-forming, horizontally spreading herb 6–14 in. (15–35 cm) tall, spreading over 4 ft. (1.2 m) across. Leaves gray-green, evergreen, oval to spatula shaped, 2 in. (5 cm) long by 3/4 in. (2 cm) wide, thick, almost succulent appearing. Flowers abundant, lilac-purple, daisylike, 2 in. (5 cm) wide, late fall to early spring.

Moderate to fast growing; space 12–20 in. (30–50 cm) apart. Fertile loam. Drought tolerant. Full sun, or full sun with a little afternoon shade. Trim back stems as they outgrow their bounds. Mow dried flowers at the end of the blooming season.

'African Queen', deeper green leaves, deep purple flowers.

'Antique Pink', pale pink petals, blue center.

'Burgundy Mound', deep purple flowers.

'Crescendo Ivory', ivory petals, blue-green center.

'Crescendo Orange', orange petals, blue-green center.

Osteospermum fruticosum
'Whirligig'

Oxalis crassipes
'Rosea'

Oxalis oregana

'Crescendo Yellow', yellow petals, blue-green center.

'Highside', rose and white bicolor petals, blue center.

'Iringa', purple petals, blue center.

'Kalanga', dark purple-pink petals, blue center.

'Lubutu', ivory yellow petals, blue center.

'Malindi', dark burgundy purple petals, dark purple center.

'Nasinga Cream', white and yellow spoon-shaped petals, creamy yellow center.

'Nasinga Pink', pink spoon-shaped petals, blue center.

'Nasinga Purple', purple spoon-shaped petals, blue center.

'Orchid', violet petals, white-ringed blue center.

'Ostica Blue Eye', white petals, bluish golden center.

'Ostica Lilac', lilac petals, golden orange center.

'Ostica White', snow white petals, yellow center.

'Riverside', yellow and white bicolor petals, blue center.

'Seaside', pink and white bicolor petals, blue center.

'Snow White' (syn. 'White Cloud'), thought to be a hybrid, showy white flowers.

'Sparkler', snow white petals, blue center, foliage edged in white.

'Volta Improved', pink and rose bicolor petals, dark blue center.

'Whirligig', silvery white spoon-shaped petals, blue center.

'Wildside', dark purple petals, blue center.

'Yellow Tulip', soft creamy yellow petals, yellow center.

Oxalis crassipes 'Rosea'
Strawberry shamrock

Great for rich shady settings. Fairly reliable in Zone 6 winters. Can be coaxed to survive in Zone 5 by properly siting it for maximum winter protection.

Only 4–6 in. (10–15 cm) tall. Leaves 1–1½ in. (2.5–4.0 cm) wide, light green, shaped like a shamrock. Flowers numerous, deep pink, ½ (12 mm) wide, taller than the foliage, early summer to fall.

Oxalis oregana
Oregon oxalis, redwood sorrel

As lush appearing as any moss or fern, Oregon oxalis looks like a giant shamrock and can be used as edging along shaded walkways and as a moderate- to large-scale ground cover underneath trees in wooded border settings. It is especially useful in naturalized gardens in the northwestern United States and as a companion to ferns and rhododendrons. Zones 7–10. Pacific Northwest coast.

A low-growing, rhizomatous herb 10 in. (25 cm) tall, spreading shyly to several feet (meters) across. Leaves 4 in. (10 cm) across, medium green, composed of three broadly heart-shaped leaflets each 1½ in. (4 cm) long. Flowers pink, rose, or white, spring, reblooming less profusely in autumn.

Slow growing; space 10–14 in. (25–35 cm) apart. Constantly moist, rich, moderately acidic soil. Moderate to dense shade. Protect from strong, drying winds. Too much sun causes the leaflets to droop and stay folded up much of the time to conserve water.

PACHYSANDRA

Among the most popular ground covers in use today, pachysandra thrives in a broad geographic range, seldom encounters serious pest or disease problems, and once it fills in can be relied upon for many years of maintenance-free service. Pachysandra should be employed on a moderate to large scale underneath trees, around shrubs, near walkways, and around building foundations. For a lovely infusion of tranquilizing lushness, try interplanting with robust blue-leaved or variegated hostas or cinnamon, lady, and royal ferns.

Well-drained, constantly moist, acidic loam. Light to dense shade.

Pachysandra procumbens
Allegheny pachysandra

A broadly clump-forming species. Leaves rough, semievergreen, medium green, sometimes silvery mottled, turning bronzy in fall. Flowers white,

*Pachysandra
procumbens*

*Pachysandra
terminalis*

malodorous, short-lived, numerous, spring. Fruit a purplish capsule, formed low on the stem, often obscured by the foliage. Zones 5–8. North America.

'**Forest Green**', leaves smaller and with consistent mottling.

Pachysandra terminalis
Japanese spurge

A semiwoody subshrub 6–12 in. (15–30 cm) tall, spreading indefinitely. Leaves more or less oval, 2–4 in. (5–10 cm) long by ½–1½ in. (12–40 mm) wide, evergreen, shiny medium green. Flowers white, pleasantly fragrant, short-lived, numerous,

spring. Fruit a white berry, produced occasionally. Zones 4–8. Japan.

Slow growing; space 6–10 in. (15–25 cm) apart.

'**Cutleaf**', deeply toothed medium green leaves.

'**Green Carpet**', more compact, slower spreading, somewhat broader leaves that are a darker and shinier green.

'**Green Sheen**', more tolerant of heat than the other selections, slow spreading with smaller, very glossy (like plastic), dark green leaves.

'**Variegata**', creamy white and green leaves.

Pachysandra terminalis
'Green Carpet'

Pachysandra terminalis
'Variegata'

Pachysandra terminalis
'Green Sheen'

Parthenocissus quinquefolia

Penstemon pinifolius

Parthenocissus quinquefolia
Virginia creeper, woodbine

This handsome, coarse-textured ground cover is primarily attractive for its foliage, which is lustrous blue-green during summer and scarlet during early fall. The standard harbinger of autumn, Virginia creeper is best suited for moderate to large plantings. It spreads quickly, shows little respect for artificial boundaries, and is especially good on shady slopes for erosion control. It also tolerates salt spray. Many bird species are attracted to the fruit. Zones 3–9. Eastern United States.

A woody, creeping vine 6–12 in. (15–30 cm) tall when unsupported, spreads indefinitely. Leaves large, five-parted, deciduous, elliptic to oval, segments up to 6 in. (15 cm) long by 2½ in. (6 cm) wide, and edged with prominent teeth. Flowers tiny, greenish white, obscured for the most part by the foliage, early to mid summer. Fruit berrylike, in clusters, green then bluish black, persisting in fall after the foliage has dropped.

Fast growing; space 30–42 in. (75–105 cm) apart. Acidic to neutral clay, sandy, or gravelly soils with good drainage. Moderately drought tolerant; needs supplemental watering only in mid summer. Light to moderate shade. Trim back the leading stems as they outgrow their bounds.

'Engelmannii', leaves smaller than the species.

'Saint Paulii', leaves smaller than the species and hairy below.

'Variegatus', leaves irregularly splashed with white.

Penstemon pinifolius
Pineleaf penstemon

Attractive to hummingbirds with its bright red tubular flowers, pineleaf penstemon is excellent in hot, low-rainfall areas, where it functions well as a general cover and soil stabilizer on flat and sloping terrain. Consider using it as a border edging, accent plant, or rock garden specimen. Zones 3–9. Southwestern New Mexico, southeastern Arizona, and adjoining Mexico.

A sprawling, low-growing subshrub 4–12 in. (10–30 cm) tall, spreading over 18 in. (45 cm) across. Leaves mostly evergreen, densely set, medium green, needlelike, ¾ in. (2 cm) long. Flowers numerous, trumpet shaped, 1½ in. (4 cm) long, yellow-bearded (due to stamens), summer.

Slow to moderate growing; space 10–14 in. (25–35 cm) apart. Neutral, gritty, moisture-retentive soils with excellent drainage. Drought and heat tolerant. Full sun.

'Mersea Yellow', yellow flowers.

Pernettya mucronata
Chilean pernettya

Good for edging paths or for moderate-scale facing near building entrances, Chilean pernettya works well as a border around swimming pools and ponds and along the banks of streams. Its primary merit is its exquisite display of colorful but poisonous fruit. Its foliage and flowers, also poisonous, are attractive as well. Zones 6 or 7. Chile, Argentina.

A low-growing, horizontally growing shrublet 18–36 in. (45–90 cm) tall, spreading over 3 ft. (90 cm) across. Leaves shiny, prominently veined, deep green, evergreen, oval to elongate, ¾ in. (2 cm) long by ⅜ in. (9 mm) wide, with somewhat toothed edges and pointed tips, turning bronzy green in fall. Flowers solitary, ¼ in. (6 mm) long, white to pink, spring and summer. Fruit round, ½ in. (12 mm) in diameter, shiny, almost metallic-appearing, white to red or lilac, long-lasting, fall to spring.

Moderate growing; space 24–30 in. (60–75 cm) apart. Moist but well-drained, acidic loam. Drought tolerant for short periods. Full sun to light shade in temperate climates; afternoon shade in very hot climates. Lightly shear lanky plants.

'Alba', white fruit slightly tinged pink.

'Cherry Ripe', big, bright, cherry red fruit.

'Coccinea', scarlet fruit.

'Dwarf Form', only 12 in. (30 cm) high by 3 ft. (90 cm) wide.

'Lilacina', lilac-purple fruit.

'Pink Pearl', lilac-pink fruit.

Pernettya mucronata

'**Purpurea**', violet-purple fruit.

'**Rosie**', red young stems, dark green leaves, pinkish rose fruit larger than the species.

'**Sea Shell**', pinkish fruit ripening to rose.

'**White Pearl**', medium to large shiny white fruit.

Perovskia atriplicifolia
Russian sage

Russian sage fills a valuable niche as a backdrop or accent plant in moderate to large areas and performs best in hot, summer climates. It is stunning in broad drifts and in the background of *Coreopsis rosea* and *C. verticillata* cultivars as well as shasta daisy (*Chrysanthemum* ×*maximum*) and white, pink, orange, or yellow forms of coneflower (*Echinacea*). It combines well with another type of orange coneflower (*Rudbeckia fulgida*) or white boltonia (*Boltonia asteroides*), and is superb in front of tall grasses. Tough, reliable, and long-lived, it offers unparalleled mid to late season color. Zones 5–9. Afghanistan to Tibet.

A subshrub 4 ft. (1.2 m) tall and wide. Leaves lanceolate to narrowly oval, sparsely toothed, prominently wavy along the edge, 1–2½ in. (2.5–6.0 cm) long by ½–1 in. (12–25 mm) wide, covered with silky hairs, bluish gray-green, on square silvery gray stems, aromatic (like menthol). Flowers numerous, tiny, two-lipped, purplish blue, mintlike, mid summer to fall.

Slow growing; space 24–30 in. (60–75 cm) apart. Acidic to neutral, well-drained soils. Drought tolerant. Full sun. Prune to 12 in. (30 cm) high after the first hard frost in fall or to the live growth the following spring.

'**Blue Haze**', paler blue flowers, leaves nearly without teeth.

'**Blue Mist**', lighter blue flowers, earlier blooming.

'**Blue Spire**', deep violet-blue flowers, deeply cut foliage.

'**Filigran**', lavender-blue flowers, finely divided lacy textured leaves.

Perovskia atriplicifolia 'Filigran'

Perovskia atriplicifolia 'Longin'

Persicaria affinis

'**Little Spire**', compact habit, very strong blooming, 25 in. (63 cm) tall.

'**Longin**', resists flopping late in the season.

Persicaria affinis
Himalayan fleece flower

Formerly listed as *Polygonum affine*, this remarkable general cover for small to moderate areas is attractive both in bloom (which may be for six full months) and out of bloom. It is effective as a facing to south or west sides of open deciduous or evergreen shrubs and small trees, and it receives high marks when planted alone in raised beds surrounded by turf. The plant may be killed back by late frost in early spring, but generally recovers in short order. Zone 3.

A mat-forming, erect-leaved, horizontally stemmed, trailing herb 4–6 in. (10–15 cm) tall, spreading to over 4 ft. (1.2 m) wide. Leaves to 4 in. (10 cm) long by 1 in. (2.5 cm) wide, more or less deciduous, narrowly oblong, edged with fine teeth, dark to medium green, becoming rusty red in fall, turning brown after a few hard frosts. Flowers numerous, tiny, faintly fragrant, in their varied patterns of pinkish, white, and rose, early summer to mid autumn.

Moderate growing; space 10–16 in. (25–40 cm) apart. Fertile soil, plenty of water, and moderate temperatures. Light to moderate shade.

'**Border Jewel**', larger foliage, blooming spring to fall.

'**Darjeeling Red**', flowers predominately dark pink.

'**Donald Lowndes**', flowers bright pink and quite showy.

Persicaria filiformis
Virginia knotweed

Formerly known as *Tovara virginica* or *Polygonum filiforme*, this rhizomatous spreading species has spawned two extraordinary ground covering cultivars. Both are colorful and interesting in woodland gardens, and are suitable for general use on a moderate to large scale. Zones 5–9. Eastern and central United States, eastern Canada, Japan.

Persicaria filiformis
'Variegata'

*Persicaria
microcephala*
'Red Dragon'

Leaves deciduous, oval to elliptic, 4–8 in. (10–2- cm) long. Flowers tiny, red, on upright to arching spikes, summer to early fall.

Moderate growing; space 12–18 in. (30–45 cm) apart. Rich, moisture-retentive soil. Protect from strong winds. Light to moderate shade.

'**Painter's Palette**', leaves mottled creamy white and green and brightly marked with a deep maroon V-shaped overlay.

'**Variegata**', leaves marbled creamy white and green.

Persicaria microcephala

Three new colorful selections of this species are nonrunning and ideal for planting next to pathways, stairs, and entryways where their every detail can be appreciated. Zones 5–9. Vigorous, clump-forming, 3–4 ft. (90–120 cm) tall by 4–5 ft. (120–150 cm) wide. Stems reddish purple. Leaves variously colored. Flowers white, insignificant, mid summer to fall.

Rich, moisture-retentive soil. Protect from strong winds. Full sun to part shade.

Persicaria virginiana
'Lance Corporal'

Petasites japonicus
'Purpureus'

Petasites japonicus
'Variegatus'

Petasites japonicus 'Giganteus'

'**Chocolate Dragon**', burgundy purple foliage with a silver V-shaped mark.

'**Red Dragon**', arrowhead-shaped deciduous leaves deep burgundy purple, maroon, and frosted green, with a silver V-shaped mark.

'**Silver Dragon**', silvery green foliage with a green edge and a red central vein.

Persicaria virginiana

A vigorous grower. Leaves overlaid with a bold mahogany chevron patch. Flowers coral-pink, on long spikes, late summer.

Moist soil. Part shade.

'**Brushstrokes**', massive velvety chartreuse-green foliage overlaid with a deep dark purplish black chevron, 2–2½ ft. (60–75 cm) tall, tiny red flowers in late fall.

'**Lance Corporal**', chartreuse green foliage overlaid with deep maroon chevrons, 1½–2 ft. (45–60 cm) tall, tiny red flowers in late summer.

Petasites japonicus
Japanese butterbur

Japanese butterbur commands attention for its unusual flowers and foliage. On vast expanses of moist, wooded terrain, it might be considered as a large-scale backdrop for woodland border plantings. Alternatively, it may be surrounded with a deep edging and used on a smaller scale. When planted along streams and ponds, the aggressively spreading root system helps stabilize banks and imparts a bold, near-tropical richness to the landscape. Once established, however, plants are difficult to eradicate. Choose a place where they will not interfere with herbs or small shrubs and combine them only with trees and large shrubs. Zones 4–9. Japan.

A stemless, robust, rhizomatous, rhubarblike perennial 3–4 ft. (90–120 cm) tall. Leaves deciduous, thick-stalked, green, kidney to heart shaped, 30–48 in. (75–120 cm) wide, edged with irregular teeth. Flowers fragrant, white to purplish, disk shaped, on stalks to 4 ft. (120 cm) tall, late winter to early spring.

Very fast growing; space 2–4 ft. (60–120 cm) apart. Moist, rich, boggy soil, but adapts to drier soils. Wilts easily, but recovers almost as fast when watered. Light to moderate shade.

'Giganteus', taller and faster spreading habit, larger leaves.

'Purpureus', 18–36 in. (45–90 cm) tall; smaller purplish leaves, yellow flowers wine-stained, preceding the foliage.

'Variegatus', 18–36 in. (45–90 cm) tall, smaller green and yellow mottled leaves, white flowers.

PHLOX

Generally, phlox are useful in rock gardens as specimens, as edging along the foreground of perennial borders, paths, or walkways, or as general covers for small areas. Often they work well as a facing to the sunny side of a low hedge or as accent plants when tucked into the cracks of a retaining wall. Wildlife gardeners value phlox for their ability to attract hummingbirds and butterflies. Zones 3–9. Eastern United States.

Moderate growing; space 10–12 in. (25–30 cm) apart. Moist but well-drained, acidic to neutral, sandy or loamy soils; *Phlox subulata* tolerates alkaline soils. Full sun to moderate shade. Mow plantings after flowering to promote a neat, compact habit. Divide every three years to rejuvenate plants and to increase flowering.

Phlox divaricata
Wild blue phlox

Makes a nice accent plant when combined with shorter ground covers. A semiwoody, low-spreading, mat-forming perennial 8–12 in. (20–30 cm) tall by 18–36 in. (45–90 cm) wide. Leaves oval to oblong, dark green, 2 in. (5 cm) long. Flowers showy, trumpet shaped, pale violet-blue to lavender, slightly fragrant, 1 in. (2.5 cm) across, mid spring to early summer.

'Charles Ricardo', star-shaped fragrant blue flowers.

'Dirigo Ice', pale blue flowers.

'Eco Texas Blue', dark purple flowers with red-violet centers.

'Fullers White', white flowers, more shade tolerant.

'London Grove Blue', compact habit, blue flowers, burgundy foliage in winter.

'Louisiana', early purple-blue flowers with magenta centers.

'Louisiana Blue', rich, dark blue flowers.

'May Breeze', pure white, highly fragrant flowers.

'Sweet Lilac', very fragrant dark lilac flowers with red centers.

Phlox subulata
Moss pink, ground pink

Perhaps the most common of the cultivated phloxes, it puts on an astounding floral show. A low-growing, mosslike, mat-forming, herbaceous species 1–2 in. (2.5–5.0 cm) tall, spreading to 2 ft. (60 cm) across. Leaves narrow, sharply pointed, evergreen, light green to gray-green, 1 in. (2.5 cm) long. Flowers numerous, trumpet shaped, red-purple to violet-purple, pink, or white, completely obscuring the foliage, 3/4 in. (2 cm) wide, mid to late spring.

'Alba', white flowers.

'Alexander's Surprise', pink flowers.

'Blue Emerald', blue flowers, compact habit.

'Blue Hills', sky blue flowers.

'Brilliant', magenta flowers.

'Candy Stripe', white flowers with pink stripes.

'Coral Eye', flowers with a halo of pink surrounding a bright coral central eye.

'Emerald Cushion', pink flowers, smaller in habit.

'Exquisite', orchid-pink flowers.

'Fort Hill', very fragrant deep pink flowers, narrower foliage.

'Keryl', blue-lavender flowers, deep green foliage.

'Millstream Daphne', pink flowers with yellow centers, vigorous growth, compact habit.

'Millstream Jupiter', blue flowers with yellow centers, compact habit.

Phlox divaricata

Phlox subulata

'Oakington Blue Eyes', vibrant blue flowers.

'Profusion', white flowers with red centers.

'Red Wings', red flowers.

'Rose Queen', blush pink flowers.

'Scarlet Flame', scarlet flowers, vigorous growth.

'Sneewittchen', pure white flowers, dwarf habit.

'White Delight', pure white, large, profuse flowers

Pittosporum tobira 'Wheeler's Dwarf'
Wheeler's dwarf Japanese pittosporum

As a low hedge along sidewalks, this cultivar is appreciated for its attractive foliage and fragrant flowers, and as a low foundation facer, its thick branches and closely set foliage completely obscure the bricks or blocks in the background. Several dozen plants can be grouped together to cover moderate to large areas. Used on a slope, this shrub is excellent for controlling erosion. Zones 8–9. Of garden origin.

A mound-forming, low-growing, compact, horizontally spreading, upright-branched, woody shrub 2–3 ft. (60–90 cm) tall by 3–4 ft. (90–120 cm) across. Leaves evergreen, densely set, leathery, oval, 2–3 in. (5.0–7.5 cm) long by ½–¾ in. (12–20 mm) wide, dark shiny green. Flowers small, creamy white, mid to late spring.

Slow growing; space 30–36 in. (75–90 cm) apart. Slightly moistened but well-drained, acidic to slightly alkaline soils. Drought tolerant. Full sun to light shade.

Polygonatum odoratum
Fragrant Solomon's seal

This species serves as an accent and specimen plant for woodland gardens but is often overlooked as ground cover for mass plantings. When several plants are grouped together in sweeping

Pittosporum tobira 'Wheeler's Dwarf' (at base of brick wall) and *Asparagus densiflorus* 'Sprengeri' (hanging over brick wall)

drifts at the back of a wooded border, they contribute a magnificent soft, motion-filled gracefulness. The springtime flowers are attractive as are the fruits that follow. At all times they appear graceful and at the slightest breeze they sway hypnotically in the wind. Zones 3–9. Europe, Asia.

A creeping perennial 18–24 in. (45–60 cm) tall, spreading to 2 ft. (60 cm) wide. Leaves elliptic to oval, medium green, 4 in. (10 cm) long by 1 1/2 in. (4 cm) wide. Flowers white, cylindrical to bell shaped, 1/2–7/8 in. (12–21 mm) long, with a yellowish green base, pleasantly lilylike in fragrance, mid to late spring. Fruit 1/3 in. (8 mm) in diameter, blue-black.

Slow growing; space 8–12 in. (20–30 cm) apart. Sandy to gravelly to loamy, acidic soils. Good drought tolerance. Moderate to dense shade.

Var. *thunbergii*, taller than the species with larger flowers and leaves.

'Variegatum', leaves edged in creamy white, Zone 4.

Polygonatum odoratum

Polygonatum odoratum 'Variegatum'

Pulmonaria longifolia

Pulmonaria
'Samouri'

Pulmonaria
'Trevi Fountain'

PULMONARIA
Lungwort

Lungworts are well suited for edging shady paths and perennial borders. Their slow rate of spread and eye-catching foliage are a splendid combination. Lungworts are very effective underneath and around deciduous shrubs and trees, and may be employed on a small to large scale.

Moderate growing; space 12–18 in. (30–45 cm) apart. Constantly moist but well-drained, rich loam. Moderate to dense shade.

Pulmonaria longifolia
Long-leaved lungwort

A low-growing, clump-forming herb 9–12 in. (23–30 cm) tall, spreading to 2 ft. (60 cm) across. Leaves narrow, dark green, with gray spots, 12–18 in. (30–45 cm) long. Flowers purplish blue. Zones 3–8. Western Europe.

'Bertram Anderson', blue flowers.

Subsp. *cevennensis*, 6 in. (15 cm) tall by 4 ft. (1.2 m) wide, with large silver-spotted leaves and dark violet-blue flowers.

'Little Blue', numerous flowers, lance-shaped leaves.

Pulmonaria hybrids
Hybrid lungwort

Numerous species and cultivars of lungwort have been crossbred to produce hybrids. These typically range from 12 to 18 in. (30–45 cm) tall. Zone 4.

'Apple Frost', compact, rose-colored flowers, apple-green leaves overlaid with silver.

'Berries and Cream', ruffled dark green leaves with silver centers, pink flowers.

'Cotton Cool', upright silver-frosted leaves, small blue flowers.

'Dark Vader', dark green leaves with silver speckles, blue-purple and pink flowers.

'David Ward', pale green leaves edged in white, salmon-pink flowers.

'Excalibur', unique narrow, silver leaves edged in dark green.

'High Contrast', predominantly silver foliage, large pink flowers age to blue.

'Majeste', uniformly silver-pewter lance-shaped foliage, pink and blue flowers.

'Milky Way', very large, heavily spotted foliage, wine-red flowers.

'Moonshine', silver foliage edged in green, pale blue flowers.

'Northern Lights', small, silvery foliage edged in light green, with cranberry, purple, and blue flowers.

'Pink Haze', green leaves splashed with silver spots, large clear pink flowers with ruffled edges.

'Polar Splash', green leaves uniformly spotted with silvery white, blue and pink-colored flowers.

'Purple Haze', compact, silvered and spotted leaves suffused with purple at the base, flowers first blue then rose.

'Raspberry Ice', large gray-green leaves edged in white, raspberry pink flowers.

'Regal Ruffles', compact, unique ruffled broadly oval, milky spotted leaves, deep lavender-purple flowers.

'Samouri', with long narrow silvery gray foliage, blue and pink flowers.

'Silver Dollar', broad, nearly round, silver leaves.

'Spilled Milk', compact, broad silvery leaves, pink flowers.

'Trevi Fountain', dark green foliage with bright silver spots; large, deep cobalt-blue flowers.

Pyracantha hybrids
Hybrid firethorn

At 8 to 12 ft. (2.4–3.6 m) tall *Pyracantha koidzumi* (Formosa firethorn) is not a ground cover, but its cultivars are. They are often used on a moderate to large scale as low, informal hedges on uneven or rocky terrain. The hybrids are colorful in flower and fruit and make great specimens. Zones 7–10.

Thorny shrubs. Leaves evergreen to semievergreen, dark shiny green, 1–3 in. (2.5–7.5 cm) long by ½ to ¾ in. (12–20 mm) wide, sometimes edged with small teeth. Flowers small, white, in clusters, not pleasantly fragrant, mid summer. Fruit small, round, becoming bright red in early fall, persisting through winter.

Moderate growing; space 3–4 ft. (90–120 cm) apart. Well-drained neutral or acidic soils.

Pyracantha 'Ruby Mound'

Ranunculus repens

Drought tolerant. Full sun. Prune upright-growing shoots as they appear.

'Red Elf', 2 ft. (60 cm) tall, mound-forming.

'Ruby Mound', 18 in. (45 cm) tall by 3 ft. (90 cm) wide, mound-forming.

Ranunculus repens
Creeping buttercup

Attractive in foliage and flower, creeping buttercup combines well with moisture-tolerant shrubs and trees. It is generally used on a moderate to large scale in naturalized landscapes.

Zones 4–9. Europe, Asia, western Canada; naturalized in northeastern United States and Canada.

A perennial herb 8–24 in. (20–60 cm) tall in moist areas. Leaves deciduous, shiny dark green, often grayish mottled, divided into three coarsely toothed, bristly haired leaflets. Flowers bright yellow, 1/2–1 in. (12–25 mm) wide, mid spring to late summer.

Fast growing; space 12–18 in. (30–45 cm) apart. Constantly moist, moderately to highly organic, acidic and alkaline soils. Full sun to mod-

Rhus aromatica 'Grow-low'

erate shade. Cut back runners as they outgrow their bounds.

'Buttered Popcorn', snowflake shaped leaves with creamy yellow centers and apple green dappling and edging.

'Pleniflorus' (syn. 'Flore-Pleno'), showy double flowers.

Rhus aromatica 'Grow-low'
Fragrant sumac

Although *Rhus aromatica* is neither showy nor popular as a ground cover (because of its size), its selection 'Grow-low' is excellent. 'Grow-low' is valuable as a salt-tolerant erosion controller for banks and slopes, especially in northern climates, and for general use in large or moderate areas, particularly along highways, in median strips, and close to parking areas. It seldom fails. 'Grow-low' generally does not combine well with other plants, but in front of tall coarsely barked trees, it makes an acceptable facing plant. Zones 3–9. Of garden origin.

A woody shrub 2 ft. (60 cm) tall by up to 8 ft. (2.4 m) wide. Leaves deciduous, miniature oaklike, glossy green, turning vibrant yellow or scarlet during autumn, oval with significant lobes along the edges, typically fragrant when crushed. Flowers yellow, appearing before the leaves begin to unfold, very early spring. Fruit red, ¼ in. (6 mm) across, late summer to early fall, often becoming brownish and persisting into winter.

Slow to moderate growing; space 42–54 in. (105–135 cm) apart. Infertile, dry, well-drained, moderately acidic soils. Drought tolerant, but welcomes an occasional deep watering during the hottest days of summer. Full sun (for best fall color) to moderate shade. Prune out branches in spring that may have broken during winter.

Rodgersia aesculifolia
Fivefinger rodgersia

Fivefinger rodgersia is great for infusing bold texture and makes a magnificent backdrop when used alone or in mass plantings. It also makes a nice specimen or accent plant, particularly near water. The leaves are outstanding. Zones 5–8. China.

A rhizomatous, perennial herb 3–6 ft. (90–180 cm) tall, usually around 4 ft. (1.2 m) in cultivation. Leaves huge, horse-chestnutlike, edged with coarse teeth, composed of seven leaflets, each 4–10 in. (10–25 cm) long, rough textured, flat to shiny medium green, on hairy petioles. Flowers petal-less, with creamy white sepals and stamens, early to mid summer.

Space 2–3 ft. (60–90 cm) apart. Rich moist soil. Light to moderate shade. Cool summer temperatures to avoid leaf scorch.

Rosa hybrids
Rose

Ground-covering roses cover the ground with style and beauty, and are useful in medium to large areas and for erosion control on sloping terrain. Many are available with long summer-blooming season, and their fruit adds late-season interest. Zone 4.

Shrubs 18–48 in. (45–120 cm) tall by 3 ft. (90 cm) wide. Leaves deciduous or sometimes evergreen, typically composed of broadly oval leaflets. Flowers very showy, colored pink, red, yellow, white, or cream. Fruit fleshy, often large, red or yellow.

Moderate to fast growing; space 30–48 in. (75–120 cm) apart. Well-drained, rich acidic to neutral soils. Fairly drought tolerant; needs an occasional deep watering in summer. Prune out

Rodgersia aesculifolia

dead or diseased stems and any upright-growing shoots immediately after flowering.

Carefree Sunshine™, upright habit, lemon yellow flowers.

Carefree Wonder™, upright habit, semidouble deep pink flowers with white centers.

Flower Carpet^PBR, more disease resistant than other roses, masses of vibrant rosy pink double flowers with a subtle fragrance.

Flower Carpet Appleblossom™, pastel pink flowers.

Flower Carpet Coral™, single coral flowers with yellow centers.

Flower Carpet Pink™, iridescent pink flowers.

Flower Carpet Red™, rich deep red flowers.

Flower Carpet White™, highly fragrant white flowers.

'**Knock Out**', cherry red flowers, resistant to black spot.

'**Lovely Fairy**', deep, vibrant pink flowers.

'**Nearly Wild**', single deep pink and white flowers, disease resistant.

Scarlet Meidiland™, 6 ft. (1.8 m) wide, semidouble scarlet flowers.

'**Snow Carpet**', 5–10 in. (13–25 cm) tall, double white flowers.

'**The Fairy**', soft pink flowers.

Rosmarinus officinalis
Rosemary

This common kitchen herb has a shrubby habit from 2 to 4 ft. (60–120 cm) tall and is only a fair ground cover, but its cultivars, which are typically more uniform in habit, sprawling, and lower growing, are quite good for this purpose. When

Rosa Flower Carpet Pink™

Rosmarinus officinalis 'Huntington Carpet'

Rosmarinus officinalis 'Prostratus'

Rubus calycinoides

single specimens or small groups are placed where their neat foliage, attractive branch patterns, and graceful trailing stems are easily viewed, they are spectacular. Other uses include turf substitution in moderate to large areas, walkway edging, dwarf hedging, and as a rock garden specimen. Zones 7–9. Mediterranean region.

Leaves leathery, hairy, grayish green, narrow, evergreen, 1/2–1 1/2 in. (12–40 mm) long, pleasantly aromatic. Flowers pale blue, rarely pink or white, about 1/4 in. (6 mm) long, spring.

Moderate growing; space 30–48 in. (75–120 cm) apart. Infertile, well-drained, acidic to neutral soils. Modestly drought tolerant. Full sun. Shear lightly after flowering to promote branching and to keep plants dense and neat looking.

'Collingwood Ingram', graceful habit.

'Huntington Carpet', very compact, mounded habit, 12 in. (30 cm) high by 4 ft. (1.2 m) wide, light green leaves, darker blue flowers.

'Irene', 6–10 in. (15–25 cm) tall, numerous violet-blue flowers.

'Lockwood de Forest', semiprostrate, mounded habit, dark blue flowers.

'Prostratus', trailing rosemary, prostrate habit, foliage and flowers like the species.

Rubus calycinoides
Taiwanese creeping rubus
Well suited to roadside plantings and as a large-scale facing for mixed tree and shrub borders, this species is also an effective soil binder on moderate to large sloping areas. Zones 6–8. Taiwan.

A low-growing, trailing, relatively woody, densely branched, thorny shrublet 2–4 in. (5–10 cm) tall, spreading over 3 ft. (90 cm) across. Leaves semievergreen to evergreen, simple, somewhat ivy shaped, deeply furrowed, shiny dark green above, lighter green below, hairy, 3/4–1 1/2 in. (2–4 cm) long and wide, turning copper-colored in fall. Flowers white, 1/2 in. (12 mm) wide, insignificant, summer. Fruit an orange base (receptacle) and a bright red-black berrylike aggregate of drupelets 1/2 in. (12 mm) long.

Moderate growing; space 16–30 in. (40–75 cm) apart. Most well-drained soils. Modest drought tolerance; requires only an occasional deep watering in hot, dry weather. Full sun. Trim back trailing shoots as they outgrow their bounds.

'Golden Quilt', new growth bright yellow before turning to green, a process that repeats throughout the growing season.

Rudbeckia fulgida
Orange coneflower
Although uninspiring when not in bloom, orange coneflower has an extended flower season that easily offsets the coarse, dull foliage of late spring and early summer. It is often confused with black-eyed Susan (*Rudbeckia hirta*). Zones 3–9. Eastern United States.

Rudbeckia fulgida var. *sullivantii* 'Goldsturm'

A rhizomatous herb 1–3 ft. (30–90 cm) tall, spreading 2–3 ft. (60–90 cm) across. Leaves deciduous, deep green, edged with teeth. Flowers daisylike, 1½–3 in. (4.0–7.5 cm) wide, with a dark brown center or cone surrounded by narrowly oval petals of vibrant buttery orange, midsummer to the first hard frost. Fruit tiny, brown, persisting into winter.

Moderate to fast growing; space 18–24 in. (45–60 cm) apart. Slightly moist, loose, rich, acidic loam. Moderately drought tolerant. Mow plantings in late winter to remove dead growth.

'Oraile', larger deeper golden yellow flowers.

Var. *sullivantii* 'Goldsturm', a popular selection with compact habit and profuse display of large vibrant flowers.

Sagina subulata
Irish moss
Although it is often overlooked in favor of taller, showier plants, Irish moss is a wonderful choice for between stepping stones or pavers and as a vibrant, lush small-scale general cover or turf substitute in coastal areas. Zones 5–10. Europe.

A low-growing, mat-forming herb 2–4 in. (5–10 cm) tall, spreading indefinitely. Leaves evergreen, thin, lance or awl shaped, ¼ in. (6 mm) long, light vibrant green. Flowers tiny, white, star shaped, solitary, highly fragrant, midsummer.

Moderate growing; space 6–10 in. (15–25 cm) apart. Rich, acidic to neutral loam. Water frequently in hot, dry weather. Full sun to light shade. When overcrowded plantings mound up, cut the mounded portion and gently press down the surrounding mat to cover up the open area.

'Aurea', Scotch moss, golden yellow foliage.

Salvia nemorosa
Sage
Formerly known as *Salvia* ×*superba*, this sterile hybrid ranges from 18 to 36 in. (45–90 cm) tall and is notable for beautiful purple flowers in early to mid summer. Zones 4–7.

Moderate growing; space 18–30 in. (45–75 cm) apart. Well-drained, gravelly or sandy, slightly alkaline to slightly acidic soils. Drought and heat tolerant. Full sun to light shade. Shear after

Sagina subulata 'Aurea'

Salvia nemorosa East Friesland

Salvia nemorosa 'Marcus'

Salvia nemorosa 'May Night'

flowering to keep plantings neat. Divide every three to four years to keep them growing vigorously.

'**Amethyst**', lilac-pink flowers.

'**Blue Hill**', lilac-blue flowers above gray-green foliage.

'**Caradonna**', purple stems, deep violet-purple flowers.

East Friesland (syn. 'Ostfriesland'), purple flowers.

'**Lubeca**', violet-blue flowers.

'**Marcus**', only 12 in. (30 cm) tall, deep purple-blue flowers throughout mid summer.

'**May Delight**', similar to East Friesland but beginning bloom in spring.

'**May Night**', blue-violet flowers from spring to fall.

'**Rose Wine**', bright green foliage, rich pink flowers.

'**Snow Hill**', snow white flowers.

'**Viola Klose**', deep violet-blue flowers.

Santolina virens
Green lavender cotton

This species makes a superb specimen in a rock garden, an excellent dwarf hedge along a walkway, and, because it is relatively resistant to fire, is often favored in public areas or as a foundation facer. Zones 7–9. Mediterranean region.

An aromatic, semiwoody, mound-forming shrub 18–24 in. (45–60 cm) tall, spreading 2–4 ft. (60–120 cm) across. Leaves evergreen, composed of tiny, hairless, beadlike dark green segments that give the plant a ferny appearance. Flowers tiny, yellow, in buttonlike heads, mid to late spring.

Moderate to fast growing; space 30–42 in. (75–105 cm) apart. Well-drained, gritty soils. Drought tolerant but needs an occasional deep watering. Full sun. Lightly shear after flowering to promote a neat, compact habit.

Saponaria ×*lempergii* 'Max Frei'
Soapwort

A popular earlier flowering cultivar, 'Max Frei' is ideal for visible locations and particularly well

Santolina virens

Saponaria ×*lempergii* 'Max Frei'

suited for edging walkways, filling elevated planters, or planting atop a retaining or terrace wall. Single specimens are excellent in rock gardens and in smaller areas, and mass plantings make splendid low-maintenance turf substitutes on sloping terrain. Zones 2–7.

A horizontally spreading to semiupright perennial 8–14 in. (20–35 cm) tall. Leaves dark green. Flowers large, carmine-pink, mid to late summer.

Moderate to fast growing; space 10–16 in. (25–40 cm) apart. Well-drained loam. Drought tolerant but a bit more vibrant if given occasional deep watering throughout the summer.

Sarcococca hookeriana var. humilis
Dwarf Himalayan sarcococca

Sometimes listed as *Sarcococca humilis*, this plant is very easy to appreciate once you see it. The problem, however, is in becoming exposed to it, for it is slow growing and difficult to propagate and therefore relatively uncommon. It produces pleasantly fragrant flowers, dark green lustrous foliage, and attractive round black fruit. Best used as a general cover or facing to trees in wooded settings on a moderate to large scale, on shady slopes it helps to bind soil and prevent erosion. Relatively tolerant of air pollution. Zones 6–9. Western China.

A low-growing, woody shrublet 1–2 ft. (30–60 cm) tall, spreading over 6 ft. (1.8 m) across. Leaves evergreen, elliptic or lance shaped, 1–3 in. (2.5–7.5 cm) long by ½–¾ in. (12–20 mm) wide, leathery, deep green. Flowers small, white, sweetly fragrant, partially obscured by the foliage, insignificant. Fruit a small, black berry, late winter to early spring.

Space 12–16 in. (30–40 cm) apart. Well-drained, rich acidic loam. Fairly drought tolerant; needs supplemental watering in extended periods of heat and drought. Moderate to dense shade. Lightly shear every other spring to encourage branching and possibly help speed the filling-in process.

Var. *digyna*, with uniform height of 2 ft. (60 cm).

Sarcococca hookeriana var. *humilis*

Saxifraga stolonifera
Strawberry saxifrage, mother-of-thousands

This well-liked, wonderfully carefree species is colorful year-round, easily cultivated, and very pleasant looking. A good general cover for small to moderate areas, it makes a splendid facing for other shade- and acid-loving plants. Sometimes it is even used as a rock garden specimen. Zones 7–10. China, Japan.

A low-growing herb 6–8 in. (15–20 cm) tall, spreading by stolons. Leaves evergreen, roundish to heart shaped, 2–4 in. (5–10 cm) long and wide, with edges often toothed and fringed with hairs, gray-green with conspicuous silvery gray veins; underside purplish maroon, warty, covered with long pink hairs. Flowers dainty, wispy, 1 in. (2.5 cm) wide, spring and summer.

Fast growing; space 10–16 in. (25–40 cm) apart. Moist but well-drained, rich, neutral to moderately acidic loam. Moderate to dense shade (particularly during the afternoon). Protect from strong, drying winds.

'Cuscutiformis', green leaves with bronze and silver veins, red stolons.

'Harvest Moon', golden leaves with maroon overlay, light pink flowers.

'Maroon Beauty', rounded deep purple foliage with platinum veins, white flowers.

'Tricolor', rose-flushed leaves variegated dark green, gray-green, and ivory white.

SEDUM
Stonecrop, sedum

Sedums are finally coming into their own in North America. This is well deserved as they require nearly no maintenance, are easy to grow, have superb drought tolerance, display beautiful flowers (and sometimes colorful fruit), and come in a variety of foliage and flower colors. All of the 600 *Sedum* species and the many times more horticultural selections can be used in sunny borders, surrounding pools or patios, along walkways, against foundations, and here and there about rock gardens and herbaceous border plantings. Fast-spreading types should be bounded by natural barriers or edging,

Saxifraga stolonifera

Sedum 'Autumn Joy'

or used as turf substitutes. The smaller species are best planted between cracks in stone retaining walls. Unless otherwise noted, the selections described below form tight mats or crowns.

The leaves vary from minute beadlike segments to broad flat oval forms. On some species they overlap, most are without stalks and attach directly to the stem, and all are succulent. The white, yellow, pink, red, or purple flowers are tiny but numerous. The fruit in some species becomes swollen and colorful. With others it simply turns brown. In either event, the mature (and later dried) flowers and fruit often contrast well with the foliage and frequently persist and add interest to the winter landscape.

Fast growing; space 6–10 in. (15–25 cm) apart. Well-drained, acidic, sandy or gravelly soil. Drought tolerant. Full sun with either afternoon or morning shade.

Sedum purpureum
Purple stonecrop
A laxly upright species 12–18 in. (30–45 cm) tall, spreading 18–24 in. (45–60 cm) across. North

Korea, Japan. Many of the cultivars are probably hybrids between this and other species or cultivars. Space 2–2½ ft. (60–75 cm) apart.

'Autumn Fire', compact habit, dusky mauve flowers.

'Autumn Joy', 16–24 in. (40–60 cm) tall, pinkish mauve to bronze-red flowers.

'Bon-Bon', early blooming, pink flowers above chocolate-colored foliage.

'Carl', deep blue-green foliage, carmine-pink flowers in late summer and fall.

'Cloud Walker', dark green foliage infused with purple-red, two-tone pink flowers in summer and fall.

'Indian Chief', like 'Autumn Joy', but with even larger flower heads.

'Jaws', deeply toothed medium green foliage, pink flowers.

'Lajos' (Autumn Charm™), leaves 5 in. (13 cm) long, blue-green with creamy yellow margin, jagged edged, drooping; mauve-pink flowers turning red as they mature.

'Matrona', fleshy blue-green foliage with red overlay, dusky pink flowers from mid summer to fall.

Sedum 'Purple Emperor'

Sedum 'Red Cauli'

Sedum reflexum

'**Purple Emperor**', deep, dark purple foliage, dusky pink flowers.

'**Red Cauli**', blue-green foliage tinted purple, bright red flowers.

'**Strawberries and Cream**', green foliage becoming purple tinged, creamy white and pink bicolored flowers.

Sedum reflexum
Spruce-leaved stonecrop

A mat-forming species 8–10 in. (20–25 cm) tall, spreading indefinitely. Leaves blue, bent backwards (reflexed), resembling succulent spruce needles. Flowers numerous, tiny, yellow, above the leaves in flat-topped clusters 1–1½ in. (2.5–4.0 cm) wide, early summer. Zone 3. Europe.

Moderate growing; space 8–12 in. (20–30 cm) apart.

'**Green Spruce**', similar but with green foliage.

Sedum spurium
Two-row stonecrop

A tight cover 2–6 in. (5– cm) tall. Leaves green, deciduous toward the base of the stems and evergreen toward the tips, taking on burgundy hues in fall. Flowers pink to purplish, star shaped, on erect stems 6 in. (15 cm) tall.

Slow growing; space 4–6 in. (15 cm) apart. Zones 3–8. Asia Minor.

'**Bronze Carpet**', robust, with bronzy, broad leaves turning deep burgundy in fall and winter.

'**Dragon's Blood**', with variably greenish and burgundy, narrower leaves turning bronzy reddish in fall and winter.

'**Elizabeth**' (syns. 'Glowing Fire', 'Purple Carpet', 'Purpurteppich', 'Red Carpet'), with bronzy purplish, broad, fan-shaped leaves that are scalloped along the margins.

'**John Creech**', pink flowers, scalloped leaves.

Sedum spurium 'Bronze Carpet'

Sedum spurium 'Dragon's Blood'

Sedum spurium 'John Creech'

Sedum spurium 'Tricolor'

'**Splendens**', somewhat larger than the species, with deep carmine flowers.

'**Tricolor**', unique for variegated foliage that is green in the center surrounded by a white border, which in turn has a pinkish purple margin, reverting to stems with entirely green leaves (which should be removed before they smother the stems with variegated leaves).

Sempervivum cultivars
Houseleeks, hen and chicks

Hen and chicks spread by producing horizontal stems that bear new plantlets (chicks) at their tips. Only the hen (main) rosette of each plant blooms. When its flowers fade, the hen rosette dies and is replaced by its chicks. In the landscape houseleeks are suitable for edging a walkway or border in a sunny location, or for controlling erosion on a sunny, sandy, gentle slope or terrace. They are excellent as foreground plants to the taller, nontrailing stonecrops, and are indispensable for filling retaining wall cracks and as rock garden specimens. Until houseleeks are used in patches of at least 3 ft. (90 cm) across, their seasonal variations in leaf color, low maintenance requirements, and drought tolerance often go unappreciated. Zones 4–8. Europe, Morocco, western Asia.

A low-growing, rosette-former 1–2 in. (2.5–5.0 cm) tall. Leaves usually oblong to oval, broad-based, with hairy edges, tip sharply pointed; blade thick, fleshly, green, blue, bronze, red, purple, orange, or gray. Flowers numerous, tiny, red, purple, yellow, or white, frequently edged with hairs, on stalks 12 in. (30 cm) tall.

Sempervivum 'Iwo'

Slow growing; space 3–5 in. (7.5–13.0 cm) apart. Any well-drained soil. Drought tolerant. Full sun to light shade. Remove the dead rosettes from main plants (which die soon after flowering) so that the chicks can more readily fill in the gaps.

'**Emerald Giant**', large rosettes of light green leaves that often turn bright orange-red in late season.

'**Godaert**', lightly fringed red leaves.

'**Iwo**', green leaves with purplish red bases and tips.

'**Lilac Time**', gray-green leaves with attractive rose overlays.

'**Maria Laach**', dark green leaves with deep mahogany tips.

'**Maroon Queen**', red-backed olive green leaves.

'**Pistachio**', bright yellowish green leaves with brown tips.

'**Red Devil**', deep purplish red leaves.

'**Royanum**', bright green leaves with dark red tips.

'**Wendy**', flat rosettes of green leaves with rose tips.

Soleirolia soleirolii
Baby's tears

An excellent carpeting plant between patio blocks and stepping stones, baby's tears is also a fine turf substitute on a small scale and an outstanding setting for statuary and bird baths. It combines well with clump-forming ferns and hostas in woodland settings and with astilbes, daylilies, and black lily-turf in sunny exposures. Despite its delicate appearance, it is a tough little plant. Zones 9–11. Corsica, Sardinia, and other islands in the western Mediterranean Sea.

A low, creeping, mosslike herb 3 in. (7.5 cm) tall, spreading indefinitely. Leaves shiny light green, evergreen, nearly round, relatively succulent, to ¼ in. (6 mm) long and just as wide, with both sides sparsely hairy, on threadlike stems. Flowers insignificant.

Fast growing; space 10–14 in. (25–35 cm) apart. Constantly moist, rich loam. Cool temperatures. Light to dense shade.

'**Aurea**', golden leaves.

Soleirolia soleirolii

SPIRAEA
Spirea

Certain varieties and hybrids of spirea are useful as ground covers because they exhibit low, mounding, dense, shrubby habits. These can be employed as specimens in rock gardens and border plantings, in mass plantings along foundations, as edgings along walkways or steps, or for accent beside boulders and statuary.

Slow to moderate growing; space 24–42 in. (60–105 cm) apart. Any well-drained acidic soil. Very drought tolerant. Full sun. Lightly shear after flowering.

Spiraea japonica
Japanese spirea

Too unpredictably shaped to be much of a ground cover, this attractive species has several superb cultivars that are 2–3 ft. (60–90 cm) tall by 3–5 ft. (90–150 cm) wide. Zones 5–9. Japan.

'Alpina' (syns. 'Nana', var. *alpina*), daphne spirea, dwarf mound-forming, 12–30 in. (30–75 cm) tall, medium green leaves, pink flowers in summer.

'Anthony Waterer', rose-pink flowers.

'Atrosanguinea', larger with deep rose-red flowers.

'Crispa', twisted coarse-textured prominently toothed leaves, pink flowers.

'Dakota Goldcharm', gold leaves with bronze tips, pink flowers.

'Fire Light', deep orange spring growth, golden yellow foliage turning red in fall, deep pink flowers.

'Flaming Mound', reddish leaves, deep carmine-red flowers.

'Flowering Mound', reddish new growth changing to yellow, dark pink flowers.

'Gold Mound', golden yellow leaves turning coppery pink in fall, small pink flowers.

'Golden Carpet', reminiscent of gold carpeting.

'Golden Elf', only 6 in. (15 cm) tall, golden yellow foliage, pink flowers.

Spiraea japonica 'Gold Mound'

Spiraea japonica 'Little Princess'

Stachys byzantina
'Helen von Stein'

'**Lemon Princess**', bright chartreuse golden foliage, pink flowers.

'**Lightening Mound**', creamy lemon new growth changing to lime, seldom flowers, best in light shade.

'**Little Princess**', larger rich green leaves, many pink flowers.

'**Magic Carpet**', orange-red to red-purple new growth changing to yellow-gold, pink flowers.

'**Neon Flash**', purple new growth changing to green, red flowers.

'**Nyewoods**' (sometimes listed as a cultivar of *S.* × *bumalda*), said by some to be identical to 'Little Princess', cheery pink flowers.

'**Shirobana**', red flower buds opening to pink and white florets carried in the same clusters.

Stachys byzantina
Lamb's ears, woolly betony

Velvety soft and shaped like lamb's ears, the light gray leaves contrast nicely with green-, purple-, and yellow-leaved perennials. Zones 4–8. Southwestern Asia.

A fine herb 4–6 in. (10–15 cm) tall, laxly spreading to 3 ft. (90 cm) wide. Leaves deciduous, 4 in. (10 cm) long, pleasantly scented when crushed, densely covered with white hairs. Flowers pink to purple, ½ in. (12 mm) long, on stalks 12–18 in. (30–45 cm) tall, mid summer until frost.

Moderate growing; space 12–16 in. (30–40 cm) apart. Constantly moist, rich loam. Moderately drought tolerant. Full sun or light shade.

Stephanandra incisa
'Crispa'

Stylophorum diphyllum

Taxus ×media
'Ward'

'Cotton Boll' (syn. 'Sheila McQueen'), compact habit, leaves slightly larger and less hairy.

'Helen von Stein' (syn. 'Big Ears'), large-leaved and nonflowering, up to 3 ft. (90 cm) tall, holds up well in heat and humidity.

'Primrose Heron', primrose-yellow leaves maturing to grayish green.

'Silver Carpet', relatively nonflowering, with thicker, woollier leaves.

Stephanandra incisa 'Crispa'
Dwarf cutleaf stephanandra

This sprawling selection functions best as a dwarf hedge, foundation facer, or soil stabilizer for moderate-sized slopes. Zones 5–9. Of garden origin.

A low-growing woody shrub 18–36 in. (45–90 cm) tall, spreading 4 ft. (1.2 m) across. Leaves deciduous, 1½–2½ in. (4–6 cm) long, bright green, with many deep irregular cuts in the margins, often reddish purple or reddish orange in fall, on downward-bowed branches. Flowers insignificant.

Moderate growing; space 30–36 in. (75–90 cm) apart. Well-drained, rich, acidic loam. Fairly drought tolerant, but may need a few deep waterings during summer. Full sun to light shade.

Stylophorum diphyllum
Celandine poppy, wood poppy

Most at home in moist shady areas where it has room to roam, celandine poppy is effective as a general cover when mass planted. Zones 4–9. Eastern United States.

An aggressive, long-blooming woodland herb 12–18 in. (30–45 cm) tall, spreading indefinitely. Leaves bluish green on yellow stems, almost succulent, semievergreen, very lush and robust, 10–15 in. (25–38 cm) long, deeply divided into five to seven lobes. Flowers bright yellow, 1½–2 in. (4–5 cm) wide, summer. Fruit an oblong fuzzy pod.

Moderate growing; space 18–24 in. (45–60 cm) apart. Any moist soil. Light to moderate shade. Give sufficient room to spread and naturalize.

Taxus ×media
Intermediate yew

This natural hybrid is popular for its countless selections which are used for facing foundations, hedges, and screens. Many of them tolerate winter and pruning very well. Zones 5–8. Taxus baccata × T. cuspidata.

A broad-spreading, upright-growing, medium to large shrub 3–4 ft. (90–120 cm) tall by 4–5 ft. (120–150 cm) wide. Leaves narrow, evergreen, needlelike, emerging light green, turning dark green, flat, about 1 in. (5 cm) long. Fruit bright red.

Slow growing; space 3–4 ft. (90–120 cm) apart. Various soil types but never permanently moist sites. Relatively drought tolerant. Full sun to moderate shade.

'Chadwickii', glossy leaves, tolerates winter well.

'Densiformis', leaves turn bronzy in fall, can be pruned.

'Everlow', only 1½ ft. (45 cm) tall.

'Sebian', very winter hardy.

'Ward' (syn. 'Wardii'), slow growing, 6 ft. (1.8 m) tall and three times as wide in 20 years.

Thymus serpyllum
Creeping thyme

Like other thymes, creeping thyme is valuable for its culinary uses as well as its colorful and pleasantly scented foliage, lovely flowers, low maintenance, and drought resistance. Thymes function well as aromatic fillers between patio blocks and stepping stones, releasing their comforting fragrances in response to the slightest step. Sometimes, and I think too infrequently, they are used as lawn substitutes or maintenance-saving general covers in small or moderate areas. Then, and perhaps at their best, they can be used for edging sidewalks and patios. Zone 4. Europe, western Asia, northern Africa.

A haphazardly sprawling herb 1–3 in. (2.5–7.5 cm) high. Leaves elliptic to oblong, dark green, ¼–⅓ in. (6–8 mm) long, slightly hairy, fragrant. Flowers numerous, lilac to royal purple, late spring to early summer.

Thymus serpyllum

*Thymus
serpyllum
'Elfin'*

*Thymus
serpyllum
subsp.
lanuginosus*

Moderate growing; space 8–12 in. (20–30 cm) apart. Infertile, well-drained, sandy or gritty, acidic to neutral soils. Drought tolerant. Full sun. Mow after flowering to keep plants neat. Rejuvenate plants that become densely woody at their bases by division and a hard shearing.

'Albus', white flowers.

'Argenteus', leaves variegated silvery white.

'Aureus', golden foliage, pink flowers.

Var. *coccineus*, scarlet flowers.

'Elfin', tightly packed small green foliage, sparse lilac flowers.

Subsp. *lanuginosus*, grayish foliage.

'Minus', less than ½ in. (12 mm) tall, gray-green leaves, white flowers.

'Roseus', pink flowers.

Tiarella cordifolia

TIARELLA

Tiarellas are a good choice for use in small clumps or on a moderate scale as a general cover or accent plant underneath deciduous trees in naturalized woodland landscapes.

Moderate growing; space 10–16 in. (25–40 cm) apart. Constantly moist, rich, acidic loam. Light to dense shade.

Tiarella cordifolia
Allegheny foamflower, false mitrewort

An attractive yet shy spreader. Leaves basal, evergreen, oval to heart shaped, coarsely textured, with five to seven lobes, 4 in. (10 cm) long, edged with uneven teeth, rich green becoming bronzy in fall. Flowers tiny, white, airy and foamlike, on thin, erect stems, mid spring. Zones 3–8. Eastern Canada, eastern United States.

'Dunvegan', pinkish flowers; deeply dissected, medium green, softly haired palmlike leaves.

'Erika Leigh', white flowers turn pink-tinged.

'Filigree Lace', lacy leaves, white flowers.

'Oakleaf', dark green oak-shaped leaves.

Tiarella ×*hybrida* cultivars

Not too many years ago the most common foamflowers available to gardeners were *Tiarella wherryi* of eastern North America and selections of *T. cordifolia*. The former remains popular, while the latter and its cultivars have largely been pushed aside by a number of their hybrid offspring, all of which are spring blooming. These range from 6 to 10 in. (15–25 cm) tall.

'Black Snowflake', deeply dissected green foliage with deep purple-black central marking, white flowers.

'Black Velvet', 14 in. (35 cm) tall, vibrant green foliage with elongated central lobe and purple veins, pink flowers.

'Brandywine', vigorous running habit, pink flowers, light green heart-shaped leaves with red centers.

'Candy Striper', green leaves with dark stripes down each lobe, white flowers.

'Dark Eyes', spreading habit, dark green maple-shaped leaves with a central wine-purple splotch, white flowers tinged pink.

Tiarella 'Eco Running Tapestry'

'**Eco Running Tapestry**', running habit, leaves deeply cut and fuzzy green with reddish black pigment extending out from their midribs.

'**Inkblot**', green leaves with a deep purple-black central splotch; many white flowers tinged pink.

'**Jeepers Creepers**', slow creeping, green foliage marked burgundy along the veins, flowers creamy white.

'**Mint Chocolate**', deeply cut foliage with a chocolaty overlay, white flowers tinted rose.

'**Neon Lights**', maple-shaped deep purple foliage with bright chartreuse green edges, flowers cream and pink.

'**Pink Bouquet**', vibrant green foliage, many pink flowers.

'**Pink Skyrocket**', deeply cut foliage with purple veins, pink flowers.

'**Sea Foam**', green foliage with purple central splotch, white flowers.

'**Slick Rock**', dark green deeply dissected leaves, pink-tinted fragrant flowers.

'**Spring Symphony**', compact green foliage with deep purple center, many pink flowers.

Tiarella wherryi
Wherry's tiarella, mapleleaf tiarella

Similar to *Tiarella cordifolia* and sometimes listed as *T. cordifolia* var. *collina*, but lacking stolons and displaying rich green, maple-shaped leaves that turn rich burgundy in fall. Flowers numerous, pinkish white, above the foliage, early summer. Zones 3–8. Eastern United States.

'**Heronswood Mist**', foliage variegated pink, white, cream, and green.

Trachelospermum jasminoides
Star jasmine, Confederate jasmine

Useful only in warm climates, whether humid or dry, this tenacious, rugged plant is best suited for moderate or large areas, particularly on sloping ground as a soil stabilizer. It grows over shallow tree roots and thus may be used as a turf substi-

Tiarella wherryi

tute or facing around tree trunks. Zones 9–11. China.

A low-growing, creeping, woody, vinelike plant 10–16 in. (25–40 cm) tall when unsupported, spreading over 10 ft. (3 m) across. Leaves elliptic to oblong, evergreen, 1½–4 in. (4–10 cm) long by ½–1 in. (12–25 mm) wide, shiny green with dark veins. Flowers white, 1 in. (2.5 cm) wide, pleasantly fragrant, mid spring and early summer.

Moderate to fast growing once established; space 18–36 in. (45–90 cm) apart. Moist, fertile, acidic loam. Needs supplemental watering during hot, dry weather. Full sun or light shade in cool climates; light to moderate shade in warm climates. Shear in early spring to promote compactness.

'Variegatum', leaves variegated green and white, sometimes with a reddish tinge.

Tradescantia virginiana
Virginia spiderwort

Virginia spiderwort is best suited for border plantings in informal landscapes on a moderate or large scale. It functions well for erosion control. Zones 4–9. Northeastern North America.

A laxly upright herb 1–3 ft. (30–90 cm) tall, indefinitely spreading. Leaves grassy, medium green, 1 ft. (30 cm) long by ½–1 in. (12–25 mm) wide. Flowers violet-purple to deep blue, 1–1½ in. (2.5–4.0 cm) wide, short-lived, typically open only in the morning, late spring through summer.

Moderate to fast growing; space 12–18 in. (30–45 cm) apart. Rich loam, including poorly drained soils. Full sun.

Trachelospermum jasminoides

Tradescantia virginiana 'Blue and Gold'

'**Bilberry Ice**', narrow leaves, soft lavender-colored flowers overlaid with brush strokes of darker lavender.

'**Blue and Gold**', bright blue flowers, chartreuse foliage.

'**Blue Stone**', dark blue flowers.

'**Carmine Glow**', deep carmine flowers.

'**Concord Grape**', rich purple flowers, frosty blue foliage.

'**Iris Prichard**', white flowers tinged with blue.

'**Isis**', Oxford blue flowers 3 in. (7.5 cm) wide.

'**Little Doll**', light blue flowers, compact foliage.

'**Pauline**', lilac-colored flowers.

'**Purple Dome**', bright rose-purple flowers.

'**Valor**', crimson-purple flowers.

Tricyrtis formosana
Formosa toad lily

Outstanding for woodlands, Formosa toad lily is best along a path where its flowers can be appreciated up close. Zones 4–9. Taiwan.

An upright-growing, rhizomatous perennial herb 2–3 ft. (60–90 cm) tall, spreading 18–24 in. (45–60 cm) across. Leaves heavily veined. Flowers orchidlike with lavender base and heavy purple spotting, late summer.

Space 2 ft. (60 cm) apart. Slightly moist to average soils. Shade to part sun.

'**Amethystina**', blue and white flowers with red spots.

'**Gilt Edge**', green foliage edged in gold, purple-spotted flowers, 16 in. (40 cm) tall.

Verbena tenuisecta
Moss verbena

Stunningly florific, moss verbena is valued for its persistent butterfly-attracting floral displays and pleasing trailing habit. It is best suited for small to medium-sized bounded areas and is striking when trailing over the edge of an elevated planter or down the sides of a raised bed. Zones 8–10. South America; naturalized from Georgia to Louisiana.

A tenacious herb 12 in. (30 cm) tall. Leaves triangular, dark green, 1–1½ in. (2.5–4.0 cm) long. Flowers blue to purple, violet, or lilac, in groups of 5 to 15, late spring through summer.

Tricyrtis formosana
'Gilt Edge', flowers

Tricyrtis formosana
'Gilt Edge', foliage

Tricyrtis formosana 'Gilt Edge', habit

Verbena tenuisecta

Veronica 'Waterperry Blue'

Moderate growing; space 12–18 in. (30–45 cm) apart. Any well-drained slightly acidic to neutral soil. Drought tolerant, although it may require occasional deep watering during the summer. Full sun. Shear lightly after the main blooming period.

'Alba', white flowers.

Veronica hybrids
Speedwell

Speedwells make good specimens in rock gardens, and if contained, are interesting along garden paths and sidewalks as edging. The shorter forms can be used between stepping stones and patio slabs, and as turf substitutes when contained in small to moderate areas. Zones 4–8.

Low-growing, tenaciously spreading perennials. Leaves deciduous to semievergreen, broadly oval to lance shaped (depending on the species), medium to deep green, either smooth or toothedged. Flowers blue, purplish, pink, or white, spring and summer.

Moderate to fast growing; space 8–12 in. (20–30 cm) apart. Slightly to moderately acidic

soils. Water regularly but do not saturate the soil. Full sun to light shade. Mow after flowering to neaten plantings and to rejuvenate growth.

'Blue Reflection', 3 in. (7.5 cm) tall, spreading several feet across, many true blue flowers in mid spring.

'Goodness Grows', 12 in. (30 cm) tall, bushy habit, blue flowers from spring to fall.

'Waterperry Blue', 4–6 in. (10–15 cm) tall, creeping habit, shiny green coppery tinted foliage, many lavender-blue flowers during early summer.

Viburnum davidii
David viburnum

A member of the honeysuckle family, David viburnum is excellent along walkways for edging and as a general cover in moderate to large areas. It also works well as an accent plant with acid-loving shrubs. It does not tolerate extremes of temperature. Zones 7–9. Western China.

A woody, mound-forming shrub 3 ft. (90 cm) tall by 4 ft. (1.2 m) wide. Leaves 2–5½ in. (5–14

Viburnum davidii

cm) long by 1–2½ in. (2.5–6.0 cm) wide, elongate-oval, sometimes edged with shallow teeth, prominently veined, evergreen, a distinct shade of dark green. Flowers small, white, not showy, in broad clusters 3 in. (7.5 cm) wide, early summer. Fruit ¼ in. (6 mm) long, bright blue, very showy.

Slow growing; space 30–36 in. (75–90 cm) apart. Constantly moist but well-drained acidic soil. Full sun to moderate shade. Lightly shear in spring to promote branching.

VINCA
Periwinkle

Periwinkles make interesting walkway edgings, shrubby border plantings, and fillers in elevated planters. Their main attributes are their cheerful flowers and their ability to blanket the ground, bind the soil, and eliminate erosion. They are at home underneath shallowly rooted trees and are so widely distributed that most people believe them to be American natives instead of the Eu-

ropean imports they are. Use them in moderate to large areas.

Fertile, rich, well-drained, acidic to neutral loam. Drought tolerant. Sun or dense shade in cool climates, with protection from dry winter winds and sun; moderate to dense shade in warm climates.

Vinca major
Big-leaved periwinkle, greater periwinkle

A low-growing, nonclimbing vinelike herb 8–18 in. (20–45 cm) tall, spreading indefinitely. Leaves oval, evergreen, 1½–3 in. (4.0–7.5 cm) long by 1 in. (2.5 cm) wide, dark green. Flowers bright blue, funnel shaped, 1–2 in. (2.5–5.0 cm) wide at the tip, early spring, often repeating in fall but less profusely. Zones 6–9. Southern Europe, western Asia.

Robust growing; space 10–16 in. (25–40 cm) apart.

Vinca major

'Alba', white flowers.

'Expoflora', blue-green leaves with irregular margins of creamy white.

'Gold Vein', green leaves with yellow centers.

'Maculata', chartreuse and green bicolored leaves with a wide margin of green.

'Morning Glory', bluish purple flowers.

'Reticulata', leaves with yellow veins (appearing to be yellow-netted).

'Variegata' (syn. 'Elegantissima'), large leaves blotched and edged in creamy white. An English selection with the same name has leaves that are smaller, thicker, and more strikingly variegated.

'Wojo's Gem', creamy yellow leaves with a broad margin of dark green.

Vinca minor
Common periwinkle, myrtle, lesser periwinkle

Among the most popular ground covers for temperate climates. A low-growing, horizontally creeping, vinelike herb 4–6 in. (10–15 cm) tall, spreading indefinitely. Leaves evergreen, oblong to oval, shiny dark green. Flowers lilac-blue, funnel shaped, ½ in. (12 mm) wide, numerous, early spring, often repeating in fall but less profusely. Zones 4–8. Europe, western Asia.

'Alboplena', double white flowers.

'Argenteo-variegata', large irregularly variegated leaves of creamy white and pale green, light blue flowers.

'Atropurpurea' (syn. 'Wine'), deep purple flowers.

'Aureo-variegata', green leaves with an irregular dull golden yellow margin.

'Blue and Gold', green leaves edged in gold.

'Bowlesii' (syns. 'La Grave', 'Bowles's Variety'), an exceptional selection; flowers more intensely blue, larger than the species, more reliable, profuse in summer and fall after the primary springtime flowering period; slower growing, less apt to root as it spreads.

Vinca minor 'Atropurpurea'

Vinca minor 'Blue and Gold'

Vinca minor 'Ralph Shugert'

Viola 'Purple Showers'

'Dart's Blue', habit similar to 'Bowlesii' but flowers a bit paler and somewhat smaller.

'Emily', large white flowers.

'Flore Pleno' (syns. 'Alpina', 'Multiplex'), double purplish blue flowers.

'Gertrude Jekyll', dainty white flowers, small leaves, trailing lower to the ground than the species.

'Gold Heart', foliage with irregular splashes of golden yellow in the center.

'Golden Bowles', leaves edged with bright yellow, large blue flowers.

'Illumination', yellow leaves edged in green, tending to revert to all green over time.

'Ralph Shugert', deep glossy green leaves with a thin white edge, flowers like 'Bowlesii'.

'Valley Glow', new growth florescent green later turning to moss green, flowers white.

Viola cultivars
Sweet violet

Although nearly all gardeners are familiar with violets, very few people consider them for a sturdy edging or general-purpose ground cover in small to moderate areas. This is unfortunate, as violets perform these tasks admirably. Usually they are best in contained areas or when given enough room to spread without harming less aggressive species. Zones 5–7. Europe, Asia, Africa.

Low-growing, tufted, rhizomatous, rather assertive leafy herbs 6–8 in. (15–20 cm) tall. Leaves evergreen, oval or heart shaped, 1–2 in. (2.5–5.0 cm) long and wide, medium green. Flowers white to rosy to various shades of purple, early spring.

Moderate to fast growing, and can become weedy; space 8–12 in. (20–30 cm) apart. Well-drained, rich, acidic loam. Water periodically in dry months. Light to dense shade; moderate to dense shade in hot climates.

'Charm', white flowers.

'Czar', deep violet flowers.

'Double Russian', small, with double purple flowers.

'Lady Hume Campbell', double lavender flowers.

'Lianne', deep violet-blue flowers.

Waldsteinia ternata

'Marie Louise', double, white to bluish lavender flowers.

'Purple Showers', large deep purple flowers.

'Queen Charlotte', deep blue flowers.

'Red Giant', large, reddish violet flowers.

'Rosina', fragrant, rose-pink flowers.

'Royal Elk', violet flowers.

'Royal Robe', large, dark purple, highly fragrant flowers.

'Silver Cloak', 10–14 in. (25–35 cm) tall, silvery green foliage.

'White Czar', white flowers and purple markings on yellow centers.

'White Queen', small white flowers.

Waldsteinia ternata
Barren strawberry

Barren strawberry is very reliable and at its best as a turf substitute for small or moderate areas, or as edging for shrub-filled or herbaceous border plantings. It also makes a good transition plant around the base of deciduous trees in a lawn as it helps to ease the change from coarse bark to fine-textured turf. Zone 4. Central Europe to Siberia and Japan.

A low-growing, mat-forming herb with a strawberry-like appearance, 4–6 in. (10–15 cm) tall, spreading indefinitely. Leaves evergreen, composed of three wedge-shaped glossy green leaflets 1–2 in. (2.5–5.0 cm) long, with irregular teeth. Flowers showy, yellow, in clusters of three to eight, atop flowering stems 8 in. (20 cm) tall, late spring to early summer.

Slow to moderate growing; space 10–16 in. (25–40 cm) apart. Rich, well-drained acidic to neutral soils. Moderately drought tolerant. Full sun to light shade.

Xanthorhiza simplicissima
Yellow-root, shrub yellow-root

This woody ground cover displays distinctly yellow roots and is excellent for moist shady sites. At home along pond and stream banks, it can be used as an edging or dwarf hedge where a deep border, sidewalk, or building foundation can keep it contained. It also functions well as a foundation facer and as a moderate- to large-scale general cover under open-canopied trees. Zones 4–9. Eastern United States.

Waldsteinia ternata, in bloom

Xanthorhiza simplicissima

A woody perennial 2–3 ft. (60–90 cm) tall, spreading indefinitely by suckers and rhizomes. Leaves deciduous, composed of three to five oval to oblong-oval leaflets, each 1½–2¾ in. (4–7 cm) long, edged with teeth, shiny medium green, becoming yellow, reddish orange, and purple for several weeks. Flowers tiny, brownish purple, star shaped, early to mid spring.

Moderate growing; space 18–30 in. (45–75 cm) apart. Moist but well-drained, rich loam. Good drought tolerance. Moderate shade.

Zauschneria californica
California fuchsia

California fuchsia, a colorfully florific native of the U.S. Southwest, is splendid as a bank cover or rock garden specimen. It thrives in drought conditions, and is valued for its colorful flowers and the hummingbirds they attract. Zones 7–9. Sierra Nevada of California.

A shrublet 12 in. (30 cm) tall by 3 ft. (90 cm) wide. Leaves gray-green, glandular, white-woolly, oval to narrowly oval, ½–1½ in. (12–40 mm) long. Flowers trumpet shaped, brilliantly scarlet, 1½–2 in. (4–5 cm) long, late summer to fall.

Moderate growing; space 2–3 ft. (60–90 cm) apart. Sandy or gravelly acidic to neutral soil. Very drought tolerant. Full sun. Remove dead stems during late winter.

Subsp. *alba*, pure white flowers.

'Catalina Form', grayer leaves.

'Compact Form', 6 in. (15 cm) tall by 18 in. (45 cm) wide, light green leaves covered with gray hairs.

'Dublin', more florific than the species.

'Etteri', low-growing, with gray leaves.

'Everett's Choice', 6 in. (5 cm) tall by 2 ft. (60 cm) wide, gray-green foliage, bright scarlet-orange flowers.

Xanthorhiza simplicissima, fall color

Zauschneria californica

Zoysia tenuifolia

'Ghostly Red', fuzzy gray-green leaves, nearly pure red flowers.

'Solidarity Pink', pinkish orange flowers.

'U.C. Hybrid', incandescent flowers.

Zoysia tenuifolia
Mascarene grass, Korean grass

Mascarene grass makes a bumpy, fine-textured, mosslike surface. Its greatest usefulness is as a substitute for turf in small to large areas or as a filler be-tween stepping stones. Typically, it is used in informal landscapes in areas that are difficult to reach with a lawn mower. Zones 9–10. Mascarene Islands.

A low, stoloniferous, mound-forming, herbaceous grass 2–8 in. (5–20 cm) tall, spreading indefinitely. Leaves evergreen, sharply pointed, bright green, 1½–3 in. (4.0–7.5 cm) long.

Slow growing; space 6–8 in. (15–20 cm) apart. Most well-drained soils. Drought tolerant. Full sun to light shade.

USDA HARDINESS ZONE MAP

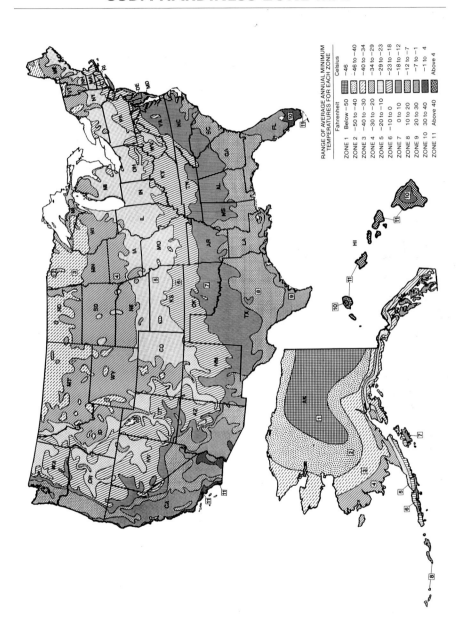

RANGE OF AVERAGE ANNUAL MINIMUM
TEMPERATURES FOR EACH ZONE

	Fahrenheit	Celsius
ZONE 1	Below −50	−46
ZONE 2	−50 to −40	−46 to −40
ZONE 3	−40 to −30	−40 to −34
ZONE 4	−30 to −20	−34 to −29
ZONE 5	−20 to −10	−29 to −23
ZONE 6	−10 to 0	−23 to −18
ZONE 7	0 to 10	−18 to −12
ZONE 8	10 to 20	−12 to −7
ZONE 9	20 to 30	−7 to −1
ZONE 10	30 to 40	−1 to 4
ZONE 11	Above 40	Above 4

EUROPEAN HARDINESS ZONE MAP

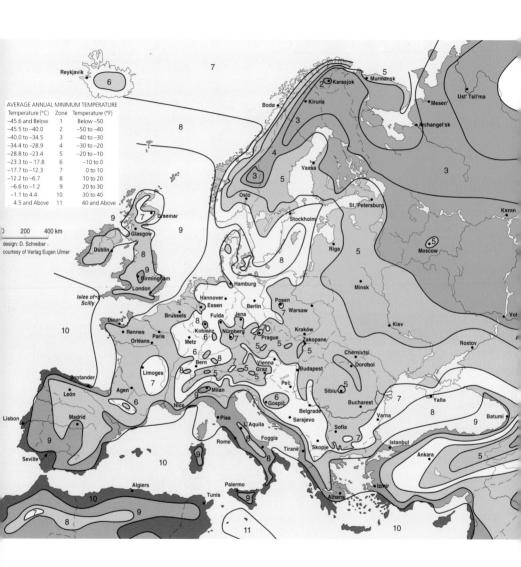

AVERAGE ANNUAL MINIMUM TEMPERATURE

Temperature (°C)	Zone	Temperature (°F)
−45.6 and Below	1	Below −50
−45.5 to −40.0	2	−50 to −40
−40.0 to −34.5	3	−40 to −30
−34.4 to −28.9	4	−30 to −20
−28.8 to −23.4	5	−20 to −10
−23.3 to −17.8	6	−10 to 0
−17.7 to −12.3	7	0 to 10
−12.2 to −6.7	8	10 to 20
−6.6 to −1.2	9	20 to 30
−1.1 to 4.4	10	30 to 40
4.5 and Above	11	40 and Above

0   200   400 km

design: D. Schreiber
courtesy of Verlag Eugen Ulmer

NURSERY SOURCES

This is a partial list, limited to nurseries in the United States, Canada, and the United Kingdom that specialize in perennials, including ground covers, or that offer hard-to-find plants. Catalogs or lists are available from most. No endorsement is intended, nor is criticism implied of sources not mentioned.

United Kingdom

Beth Chatto Gardens
Elmstead Market
Colchester
Essex C07 7DB
44 (0)1206 822007
http://www.bethchatto.co.uk

Primrose Bank
Redroofs
Dauby Lane, Kexby
York YO41 5LH
44 (0)1759 380220
http://www.primrosebank.co.uk

United States

Arrowhead Alpines
P.O. Box 857
Fowlerville, Michigan 48836
(517) 233-3581
http://www.arrowheadalpines.com

Blanchette Gardens
267 Rutland Street
Carlisle, Massachusetts 01741
(978) 369-2962
http://www.blanchettegardens.com

Bluestone Perennials
7211 Middle Ridge Road
Madison, Ohio 44057
(800) 852-5243
http://www.bluestoneperennials.com

Collector's Nursery
16804 NE 102nd Avenue
Battle Ground, Washington 98604
(360) 574-3832
http://www.collectorsnursery.com

Deer-Resistant Landscape Nursery
3200 Sunstone Court
Clare, Michigan 48617
(800) 595-3650
http://www.deerxlandscape.com

Emory Knoll Farms
3410 Ady Rd.
Street, Maryland 21154
(410) 452-5880
www.greenroofplants.com

Ensata Gardens
9823 E. Michigan Avenue
Galesburg, Michigan 49053
(269) 665-7500
http://www.ensata.com

Forestfarm
990 Tetherow Road
Williams, Oregon 97544
(541) 846-7269
http://www.forestfarm.com

Garden Vision
63 Williamsville Road
Hubbardston, Massachusetts 01452
(978) 928-4808
http://www.home.earthlink.net/~darrellpro

Goodwin Creek Gardens
P.O. Box 83
Williams, Oregon 97544
(800) 846-7359
http://www.goodwincreekgardens.com

Greer Gardens
1280 Goodpasture Island Road
Eugene, Oregon 97401
(541) 686-8266
http://www.greergardens.com

Heaths and Heathers
502 E. Haskell Hill Road
Shelton, Washington 98584
(800) 294-3284
http://www.heathsandheathers.com

Heronswood Nursery
7530 NE 288 Street
Kingston, Washington 98346
(360) 297-4172
http://www.heronswood.com

Highland Heather
8268 S. Gribble Rd.
Canby, Oregon 97013
(503) 263-2428
http://www.highlandheather.com

Oakes Daylilies
P.O. Box 268
Corryton, Tennessee 37721
(800) 532-9545
http://www.oakesdaylilies.com

Plant Delights Nursery
9241 Sauls Road
Raleigh, North Carolina 27603
(919) 772-4794
http://www.plantdelights.com

Plants of the Southwest
3095 Aqua Fria Road
Santa Fe, New Mexico 87507
(800) 788-7333
http://www.plantsofthesouthwest.com

Primrose Path
921 Scottdale-Dawson Road
Scottdale, Pennsylvania 15683
(724) 887-6756
http://www.theprimrosepath.com

Roslyn Nursery
211 Burrs Lane
Dix Hills, New York 11746
(631) 643-9347
http://www.roslynnursery.com

Roycroft Daylily Nursery
942 White Hall Avenue
Georgetown, South Carolina 29440
(800) 950-5459
http://www.roycroftdaylilies.com

Shady Oaks Nursery
1601 5th Street SE
Waseca, Minnesota 56093
(507) 835-5033
http://www.shadyoaks.com

Siskiyou Rare Plant Nursery
2825 Cummings Road
Medford, Oregon 97501
(541) 772-6846
http://www.siskiyourareplantnursery.com

Songsparrow Nursery
13101 East Rye Road
Avalon, Wisconsin 53505
(800) 553-3715
http://www.songsparrow.com

Variegated Foliage Nursery
245 Westford Road
Eastford, Connecticut 06252
(860) 974-3951
http://www.variegatedfoliage.com

Wayside Gardens
1 Garden Lane
Hodges, South Carolina 29695
(800) 845-1124
http://www.waysidegardens.com

White Flower Farm
P.O. Box 50, Route 63
Litchfield, Connecticut 06759
(800) 503-9624
http://whiteflowerfarm.com

Yucca Do Nursery
P.O. box 907
Hempstead, Texas 77445
(979) 826-4580
http://www.yuccado.com

Viette, Andre, Farm and Nursery
P.O. Box 1109
Fishersville, Virginia 22939
(540) 943-2315
http://www.viette.com

Weird Dude's Plant Zoo
1164 Frog Pond Road
Staunton, Virginia 24401
(504) 886-6364
http://www.weirddudesplantzoo.com

GLOSSARY

annual a plant that completes its life cycle in a single season

basal of the base of a plant

bracts leafy appendages

compound leaf a leaf that is composed of two or more leaflets

corolla the inner whorl (usually of petals) that surrounds a flower

cultivar a plant variety that originated in cultivation

double flower a flower with twice the usual number of petals

erect having an upright growth habit

evergreen having leaves that remain attached throughout the year

fleshy pulpy or juicy at maturity

floret a tiny flower

fruit the structure that comes from the ovary of a flower and encloses the seeds

habit the typical form, shape, and mode of growth that a plant exhibits

habitat the conditions, such as climate, soil, and light, under which a plant grows

herb, herbaceous herblike, not woody

hybrid a plant that arose from cross-pollination of two or more types of plants

loose with an open habit of branch arrangement

margin the leaf edge

mossy displaying a matted, low habit of growth—resembling that of a moss

needle a slender, often pointed leaf, like that of a conifer

nodding drooping or bending over, usually in reference to flowers

oblong longer than wide with one end wider than the other

perennial any plant that lives for three or more years

petal the single unit of a floral corolla

pod a fruit that is beanlike in shape

prostrate lying flat on the ground, normally in reference to the stems or overall habit of a plant

rhizome, rhizomatous a horizontally spreading underground stem that often sprouts up and forms a new plant at its tip

rosette a group of leaves that encircles a stem

runner a horizontally growing shoot (stolon) that typically gives rise to a plantlet or plantlets at its tip

seed the structure that arises from a fertilized ovule and contains an embryo and a food supply

semievergreen fully holding only a portion of the leaves throughout the year

sepal a leaflike part of the whorl of leaves that protect a flower

shrub a woody plant that is generally lower growing than 14 ft. (4.2 m) and has a tendency to produce many branches

shrublet a small shrub

silky covered with soft fine hairs

solitary occurring alone

spike an unbranched, elongate type of inflorescence

stamen the male reproductive apparatus composed of an anther and filament

stolon a horizontally oriented, aboveground stem (runner) that roots from, or produces plants at, its tip—as in strawberries

subshrub a shrub in which the stems are woody but terminal new growth is killed back each year

texture the overall effect or impression displayed by a plant, often listed in terms of soft, rough, coarse, or smooth.

toothed having teethlike projections

trailing horizontally growing but not rooting as it spreads

tufted a type of habit whereby the leaves are held tightly together, originate from a single point at the plant's base, then flare outward

vine a trailing or climbing plant with limp stems

FURTHER READING

Armitage, Allan. 1997. *Herbaceous Perennial Plants: A Treatise on Their Identification, Culture, and Garden Attributes*. 2d ed. Champaign, Illinois: Stipes Publishing Company.

Armitage, Allan. 2000. *Armitage's Garden Perennials: A Color Encyclopedia*. Portland, Oregon: Timber Press

Armitage, Allan. 2004. *Armitage's Garden Annuals: A Color Encyclopedia*. Portland, Oregon: Timber Press.

Brenzel, Kathleen, ed. 1995. *Western Garden Book*. Menlo Park, California: Sunset Books.

Dirr, Michael. 1998. *Manual of Woody Landscape Plants*. Champaign, Illinois: Stipes Publishing Company.

Halpin, Anne, ed. 2001. *Northeastern Garden Book*. Menlo Park, California: Sunset Books.

Jelitto, Leo, and Wilhelm Schacht. 1990. *Hardy Herbaceous Perennials*. 3rd ed. Portland, Oregon: Timber Press.

MacKenzie, David. 1997. *Perennial Ground Covers*. Portland, Oregon: Timber Press.

Rice, Graham, and Strangman, Elizabeth. 1993. *The Gardener's Guide to Growing Hellebores*. Portland, Oregon: Timber Press.

INDEX